PS
DER

ourney – from Dundee
on via South Shields,
oldham, Bradford, Bethnal
e Rhondda Valley and
nder the skin

ce...
ed, he will sa...
of the themes that shap...
are drizzled in
gar. Chippies have
working clas...
quality f...
regio...

OD OF THE

Ther   of every town
nd   here the ai
s.   nd thic
                        It is
              ow   have sp
                          the   last
                          investigates the s...
                          ciable – history of fish
                          revealing the s...
                          at bind us to this...

10

'Chippy
tea...

Food s...

FOOD
OF THE
CODS

HOW
FISH & CHIPS
MADE
BRITAIN

FOOD
OF THE
CODS

DANIEL GRAY

Harper
North

HarperNorth
Windmill Green
24 Mount Street
Manchester M2 3NX

A division of
HarperCollins*Publishers*
1 London Bridge Street
London SE1 9GF

www.harpercollins.co.uk

HarperCollins*Publishers*
Macken House, 39/40 Mayor Street Upper
Dublin 1, D01 C9W8

First published by HarperNorth in 2023

1 3 5 7 9 10 8 6 4 2

A catalogue record for this book
is available from the British Library

HB ISBN: 978-0-00-862888-8

Printed and bound in the UK using 100%
renewable electricity at CPI Group (UK) Ltd

This book is produced from independently certified FSC™ paper
to ensure responsible forest management.

For more information visit: www.harpercollins.co.uk/green

To blue eyes, who always nicks a chip
on the way home.

CONTENTS

INTRODUCTION

I would not be alive if fish and chip shops had never existed. Early in the 1920s, Laura March, not yet out of her teens, was working in the family chippy on Bank Street in Wetherby, near Leeds. In the queue that evening waited Fred Gray, a miner from Aberford, 8 miles down the road. Eyes met over the frying range, courting sizzled into marriage and my grandad was born in 1925.

It would be opportune to say that this tale spurred my lifelong love of all things fish and chips, but in fact I discovered it only while writing this book. Instead, I remember Laura – my great-grandmother – for three things: that we called her 'Granny Grunt' for being miserable; that she lived on Parson's Green where the street sign's letter 'P' always used to go missing; and that she would always Sellotape a £1 coin in the left-hand corner of birthday cards (which, incidentally, she signed 'Granny Grunt').

This, though, is not some kind of family memoir – we are not interesting enough, just *very* Yorkshire. Childhood memories do occasionally meander across its pages, as is probably inevitable for most of us when it comes to fish and chips. The dish carries a sentimental weight, and a happy one. It is part of our collective and individual folklore and identity – those lost chippies we fondly recall from the past, or a side dish or sauce particular to the area we grew up in but left.

What follows is a book written from Fred's side of the counter rather than Laura's. It is about the delights of being a customer and a diner, although every story told and place visited is underpinned by owners, fryers, servers and the glorious shops they keep.

This is for those of you who know the joy of a parent declaring 'Chippy night!', of seeing the golden glow of a chip shop on a dark evening, or of feeling a sudden pang of hunger when in range of its blissful scents. It is about piles of bread rolls (or cobs or baps or whatever they're called where you're from) on the counter beside giant jars of pickled things; about wooden forks, polystyrene tubs of mushy peas the colour of snooker tables, and fridges of fizzy drinks rarely seen in other places; and about answering the key questions of 'Salt and vinegar?' and 'Open or wrapped?' It is about eating outside on a cold winter's night, cradling the paper's warmth, or sneaking a chip on the way home.

I wanted to write an homage to those feelings and experiences, as well as answer questions and seek out the endearing idiosyncrasies of chippies. For example, I knew scraps – gorgeous tiny clippings of batter off-cuts scooped from the frying range and sprinkled on chips or munched alone – are not served in Scotland, but where is their southern border? I had a desire to learn about (and, yes, taste) the many regional variations of food on offer from chip shops across Britain.

And I wished to sketch out the dish's social history, showing how chippy culture has influenced us and been swayed by its surroundings. In the debated story of how fish and chips came to be can be found themes of immigration, race, war, class, women's equality and local and national identity. Among these wider narratives sit the parts of history I love most: the anecdotes of Geordie kids using their gasmasks to hold fish and chips or a Humberside chippy vending machine operated by a man pretending to be a robot.

This book is not a comprehensive history, of which there have already been two extremely valuable versions (Professor John K. Walton's *Fish & Chips & the British Working Class* and *Fish and Chips: A Takeaway History* by Professor Panikos Panayi.) Nor is it a guide to the finest chippies, a delve into the sustainability of fishing or a survey of potato types. At no point do I address health or dietary concerns; when chippy night is called, all that must go out the window. Look away now if you're expecting the work of a food critic: the book does not contain restaurant reviews and I have eschewed pointed nitpicking of chippies and their products. Theirs is a hard enough job without some amateur possessing an unhealthy obsession with scraps putting the boot in. Of course, I have had bad fish and chips, sometimes in researching this book, but this is fundamentally a celebration.

The sense of this being an arduous trade to operate was especially true in the period when I undertook my travels. A combination of post-Brexit supply chain difficulties, a shortage of cheap raw materials resulting from the war in Ukraine and severe energy cost rises made running a chip shop more difficult than ever. Consequently, chippies were closing at a saddening and alarming rate; the National Federation of Fish Friers warned of 'potentially an extinction event for small businesses'. For customers, the central repercussion was a stark increase in the price of this traditionally affordable treat. Even takeaway fish and chips had, in many places, climbed above the psychologically sacrosanct £10 barrier.

This troubled backdrop provided compelling motivation for travelling and writing. More than ever, I felt a determination to cherish and champion this food and these places. I wanted to let daylight in upon magic, considering and then explaining the sorcery behind fish and chips, and to show that our chippies retain resilience and vigour. This would be a love letter, not a eulogy. Moreover, it is far from controversial to assert that our country's recent past has been somewhat fractious. In something as seemingly frivolous as fish and chips, I saw an emblem – and an industry – that symbolised shared belonging and collectivism. In a time of so much sound and fury, this had to be a story worth pursuing.

Although my journey for the book started on the east coast of Scotland, my chippy Odyssey really began in the North Yorkshire village I grew up in, Copmanthorpe. As a child, my friends and I would sit on a low wall outside Bill's. No food tasted so divine as the scorching fish and chips we ate on those cold evenings, often as a second sneaky tea, steam rising into the black sky. There followed other pillar and staging-post chippies. After Middlesbrough football matches, my dad would take me to the Essex Street shop in that town, its windows forever glazed with fried heat. 'Any fish tonight?' the fryer would ask as we entered, always a good sign – along with a queue – as it meant freshly prepared food. When I later became a dad myself, going for fish and chips came to be something my daughter and I did together from a very young age. She is a teenager now, but still a wave of preposterous pride washes over me when she begs for a trip to the chippy.

Here, then, is one man's take during a looped journey across Scotland, England and Wales in the spring and summer of 2023. There will be omissions; readers may well sigh in disbelief that their beloved chip shop or speciality dish has been missed. Therein, though, is the charm of this meal: we care about it with an almost alarming intensity.

This book is an attempt to recapture that village wall feeling several times over, without significant weight gain. It is an expression of what fish and chips mean to me, and to so many of us. Few places feel as promising as the queue outside a chippy. This book ponders why. Pass the salt, will yer?

1.

PEA BUSTERS AND GRAMPIAN TEMPURA

Dundee and Stonehaven

As the train shuffled towards Dundee, its conductor made a confession. The forty-something man had one great regret, he said, about having moved from Grimsby to rural Aberdeenshire. 'They don't batter their fishcakes,' he told a couple of pensioners. 'Imagine that!'

The pair looked as if this remarkable concept was indeed within their powers of imagination, and so he continued. 'I went into the chippy, I said: "You've got batter. You've got fishcakes. Please batter a fishcake for me."' His plea had initially been met with resistance. '"We don't do that here," they said' – before a deal was brokered. 'Now, as soon as they see me coming in on a Friday, they batter two for me.' It was clear that this mattered to the conductor and had even played a small part in helping him resettle. A taste of his old home had made him feel more comfortable in his new, batter acting as a soother and a lasso dragging Humberside and Aberdeenshire closer.

It surprised me that a Scottish fish and chip shop would not normally batter its fishcakes. After almost two decades of living north of the border, I had concluded that there was no foodstuff these outlets would not smother and then deep fry. To look into the display cases of frying ranges here is to see a bronze and flaxen menagerie of edible breeds in shapes oblong and octagon, triangle and tubular. Sometimes, haddock lounge among them, left to bathe in the luminous heated light all day so that their ends curl up like those of Christmas cracker fortune-telling fish in the palm of a hand.

Other battered species include: burgers of beef and chicken; sausages jumbo and small or smoked and saveloy; white pudding and black pudding, and occasionally something called red pudding; haggis and king ribs and mock chops and chip steaks; fritters of potato and pineapple, spam and polony; onion rings, pakora and margherita pizzas. This tendency to cloak so many items in batter, as if assimilating them into one crispy family, has become ingrained in Scottish culture. 'Deep fry your pizzas / We're gonna deep fry your pizzas,' sang members of the Tartan Army when travelling to watch the Scotland national football team play in Italy during the 1990s.

My early impressions of Scottish fish and chip shops – or 'fish and chicken bars' as they were, and are, commonly subtitled – echoed this ethos of choice and variety. The chippies I had grown up with in Yorkshire offered a limited and spartan single-board menu of fish, sausages and the odd wildly hedonistic extra such as a potato scallop. Here, entire walls were required to catalogue the exotic offerings, with each item accompanied by two prices: 'single' or 'supper'. That word 'supper' summoned two confusing interpretations – firstly, of a pre-bedtime bowl of Shreddies in front of the telly as a child, and secondly, what I'd heard well-spoken people call their tea. Neither impression – perhaps drawn from both ends of the social class spectrum – proved correct. 'Supper' simply meant 'with chips'.

This bountiful approach extended beyond the frying ranges. There, hoarded on neatly curated shelves, were shimmering chocolate bars and sweets, biscuits and bubble gum. Next came sentry lines of cigarettes and Rizla papers, four-packs of lager and half-litres of vodka, then blended whiskies and wines no-one was ever drunk enough to try. In whirring fridges, glass bottles of Irn-Bru, Red Kola, limeade and cream soda were accompanied by more widely-spotted cans of pop – or 'juice' here, and sometimes 'ginger' – and milkshakes.

Arriving in Scotland after a lifetime of chippies in which retailing both Vimto *and* Tizer counted as edgily excessive made you feel like a Soviet-era Muscovite recently deposited in New York. As if all of that were not discombobulating enough, and contrary to this country's apparent batter epidemic, another bewitching fact struck me: Scottish chippies neither made nor offered scraps. Scraps, those brittle dreamy morsels of delight. Scraps, a form of edible confetti perfect for scattering over chips. Scraps, that joyous ballast to be loaded into a vice made from buttered slices of white bread. I wondered how I could ever settle in such a barbaric nation.

Outside Dundee railway station, two men in suits were engrossed in their own voices. 'The problem with Paul,' said one of them, 'is that when he does that, he makes a bridge for his own back.' This overheard snapshot took place just a few days after I'd heard someone claim that 'every God has its day', and I now dearly hoped that our flummoxed post-Covid era brains were about to usher in a golden era of mangled aphorisms.

From the Victorian era onwards, Dundee was a place of mill and dock workers, and a rebellious one too. This was Scotland's Suffragette City, where the local MP – and convinced fish and chip loyalist – Winston Churchill faced regular haranguing. Among other instances, he was chased through the streets, forced to give a speech from a shed and subjected to a bell being rung every time he opened his mouth. Most vociferous of all Dundonians were the women mill-workers whose job it was to comb out jute before it could be spun. This nasty, dark and dangerous role was known as 'heckling'. It was for them and their vehement protesting that the word took on its modern meaning. In 1911, even young children revolted in the name of progress – 1,500 of them walked out of their classrooms in a strike against corporal punishment, hurling rocks at school windows.

A population who spent so much time outdoors – walking to the mill, picketing outside it, heckling at public meetings

– and had little room for domestic niceties required a rapid, filling and cheap source of sustenance. It took a Belgian to calculate this and provide them with what they needed.

Born in 1847, Edward de Gernier had survived a shipwreck before he arrived on the east coast of Scotland in the 1870s. For a while he became a millworker, then resumed his former trade of repairing shoes. As de Gernier strolled the streets of his adopted city, he was struck by the absence of a culinary delight that was a working-class staple in his native Molenbeek: the chipped potato.

Inspired by this revelation, de Gernier spent his miserly savings – thruppence in all – on a rented space in Dundee's Greenmarket arcade. He then procured a brazier and a pan, a vat of mutton fat and a sack of potatoes. On a Friday evening in 1874, one of Britain's earliest chip shops opened for business. More than 400 portions were sold that shift; the rebels and hecklers had found their ideal nourishment.

Beneath a canvas tent roof, de Gernier's Dundonian customers would perch upon discarded wooden crates as they awaited and then devoured their exotic refreshments, a cooking pot babbling away in the background. The Belgian's stall became a social hub, full of gossip and plotting. Soon, the great importer diversified – customers could now opt to have mushy peas that had been doused in vinegar sprawled across their chips. The dish quickly became known as a 'Pea Buster', with 'buster' being a term relating to flatulence, the apparent result of its consumption. It was said that people visited Dundee just to sample a Pea Buster, with some walking beside the River Tay all the way from Perth, 20 miles away.

The secret to de Gernier's sublime chips was, said his grandson – also Edward – in 1990, his patient treatment of potatoes: 'They sat in the water for two or three days before they were peeled and, by that time, the starch was all out of them and lying in a thick layer at the bottom.' As a child, Edward remembered cutting potatoes for his grandad in what had become the family trade. At one point, the de Gerniers ran six Buster stalls, as they came to be known, though they never expanded beyond Dundee. For the pair of them, working together was not always tranquil. Under the headline 'Brotherly Love in the Greenmarket', a *Dundee Courier* story in November 1892 detailed how one de Gernier son – Edward, again – had been found guilty of assaulting his brother, Anthony, as they packed away their stall. For 'striking him on the back of the head with his fist', Edward was fined 10*s*.

When their mother, Julia, died a decade later, the bereaved Edward retired from bustering and returned to the shoe trade. He worked until he died, aged 79, in 1926. De Gerniers continued to run Buster stalls and chip shops until the 1960s, at which point their presence melted into the menu boards of other families' chippies – Pea Busters are still served in Dundee now.

De Gernier's delicacy had first fed this city's rambunctious workers, before becoming a sacred fragment of Dundonian social life. Buying a bottle of sarsaparilla from the chemist, waiting as a white-aproned fryer ladled molten peas onto chips and then gorging this al fresco meal was a ritual many thousands of locals anticipated every week. The Belgian ingrained chips into local life. By 1947, the *Dundee Evening Telegraph* claimed that the city's fish and chip shops provided 18 million meals a year, although 'A peculiar feature of the trade in Dundee is the number of chips-only orders as compared with fish suppers. The ratio is about four to one, which provides a striking comparison with English towns of similar size ...' De Gernier's influence lasted way beyond his passing, perhaps.

Leaving the suited men to their bridges and backs, I walked down The Greenmarket in search of a Pea Buster. The only food available on the site of de Gernier's stall now is roadkill – this area was tarmacked and given over to motor vehicles many years ago. Through frizzy, irritating rain I walked for a while until catching the glow of a chippy beaming across the street, its lit frying range like a landing strip after a turbulent flight. Inside, I found a menu offering both a Pea Buster and a Bean Buster, and an old man sitting at a table by the till, resting while his order was prepared. 'There you are, Tommy,' said the man behind the counter before handing him a piping hot bundle swaddled in white wrapping paper.

'What can I get ye'?' he asked abruptly while moving back towards the till. His manner reminded me of a riled swan hissing away at a bread-bearing toddler. Because there are few funnier things than trying to make a surly person say the word 'fart', as The Swan concocted my Pea Buster I risked a pecking by asking 'Why is it called a Pea Buster?' 'Dunno,' he said, 'Just is. Bean Buster. Pea Buster. I've no idea. Do you want salt 'n' vinegar on this?' In one last effort at healing this rift between Yorkshireman and Dundonian, I asked what the recipe was: 'Just mushy peas from a tin. I'd no' eat it.'

Outside the shop I began to retrospectively enjoy my conversation with The Swan. His grumpiness and disinterest pleased me – why should everyone encountered on this journey share my fish and chip romanticism or answer my annoying questions? Customer service and those interactions at the counter would and should vary between every single chip shop. Just as no two were the same in signage or furniture, neither were there agreed dialogue protocols or friendliness standards as would be found in a sterile burger chain. The Swan was part of the greasy tapestry.

I unravelled the Pea Buster, in reality a foam tray of tepid mushy peas sploshed over pale chips. The sky leaked onto this unmoving green sludge, a neon toupee over a bumpy scalp. I ate a few mouthfuls, dumped the rest in a bin outside a vape shop, and along the Tay in Broughty Ferry Edward de Gernier turned in his grave.

Like de Gernier's dish, Scotland's most famous modern battered product does not contain any fish. The Deep-fried Mars Bar, though, was motivation enough for a brief detour north in search of dessert. Stonehaven, a pretty and finely set harbour town 17 miles south of Aberdeen, is its birth-place.

In the summer of 1992 – that half-modern year of John Major, *Ghostwatch* and 'Rhythm is a Dancer' – two teenage schoolboys scuffed their way towards the Haven Fish and Chip Bar on a corner end of Allardice Street. John Davie and Brian McDonald were having the kind of blissfully pointless conversation that young people should, debating whether chocolate bars, and which ones precisely, could be deep fried in batter. One wagered the other that he would not eat a battered Mars bar, then both asked Evelyn Balgown, that day's Haven frier, to make one for them. She gained permission from her boss – the owner, Ingram Mowat – and the experiment began.

'I just dunked it in the batter and chucked it in the frier,' Evelyn told a newspaper at the time. 'The batter stopped the chocolate melting and the result was crispy on the outside and gooey on the inside.' John and Brian adored the sensation and taste. Word spread and children swarmed to the Haven, many brandishing Snickers or Crunchie bars and demanding that they too be given a batter makeover. 'I draw the line at popping their wine gums and Chewitts into the fat,' added Mowat. Soon, chippies across Scotland began to cook and sell their versions, and the deep-fried Mars bar became a tourist attraction.

Passing gardens of cheery muscari and swaying tulips, I made my way to The Haven, nowadays named The Carron after the slender river it stands beside. With not a child in sight a lollipop man rested against a low wall, a shepherd lacking his flock. 'How are you?' I asked. 'Oh, you know,' he replied, 'busy. Well, I'd like to be.' This peaceful town, with its natural harbour and heated lido swimming pool, and its local butchers, stationers and bakery, is not a place that fits the popular stereotype of the deep-fried Mars bar. In the minds of many and the column inches of some, that snack became a symbol of decay and of urban poverty and ill-health. Yet Stonehaven is so affluent that it even has open and functioning public toilets, a beacon of luxury in contemporary Britain.

Regardless of its origins, the battered Mars became simultaneously a segment of Scottish identity and an unwanted slur on the national character and diet. Which of those it was depended on who you asked, and it was possible for the same person to hold both viewpoints at once. The most common opinion among my Scottish family and friends, though, was far less complex: 'I've never tried one. They look disgusting.'

The Carron Fish Bar's pebbledash walls are the colour of well-used sandpaper and it is hatted by a steep slate roof. 'Birthplace of the World-Famous Deep-Fried Mars Bar' boasts a banner above one of its windows. A merry welcome reached me from the woman behind the counter and was sustained by the genial interior of her shop. The Carron is a modern room, its frying ranges displaying time countdowns on digital monitors ('Scampi 00:49'; 'Mars Bar 01:33') and a large screen showing videos and listing credentials ('Gluten free options available'). This, together with its pristine blue and white tiles, gave it the aura of a marine technology exhibition room in a sea life centre, a far from unpleasant look.

I experienced a sense of guilt asking for a deep-fried Mars bar, as if ordering would provoke a telling off from the friendly lady. Those tabloid tales of sloth and angina had obviously permeated my conscience. It felt shameful and contraband, and I whispered my request in the manner of someone looking to obtain off-ration bacon. Of course, such illicit dealings were merely everyday conversation to her – in the height of the summer tourist season The Carron serves up to 200 battered Mars bars every week. She simply replied: 'Is that a Supper or on its own?'

Down at the harbour I sat on a bench and unfurled the paper bag containing this Grampian tempura. The deep-fried Mars bar seemed to cower in the corner like a shy rescue dog and had become firmly lodged there by a glue of seeping caramel. Only then did it occur to me that I had no idea how this delicate, gloopy bullion should be consumed. To drag it from the bag would cause collapse. Cutlery was out of the question and would surely incur cackles from locals and seagulls alike. In the end, I tore away the paper in the manner of a paramedic removing clothing at an accident scene and held up my prize. It looked a bit like the remains of an animal that had been burned unidentifiable in an Australian bush fire. It tasted ridiculously, absurdly heavenly. The batter sleeping bag bore the rough pocks of the moody North Sea I now looked out to. The Mars' interior mash resembled some form of brunette lava. Eaten together, they were a conjuring trick and a marvel, an honest kind of decadence. Brian and John: you changed the world.

There is Renato's in Dingwall and Val Di Vara in Brechin. There is Marco's in Arbroath and Iannarelli's in Forfar. There is Mordente's in Tayport and Nico's in Clackmannan. Kirkcaldy has La Valente and Cowdenbeath Dario's. Queensferry has Graziano's and Armadale Coia's. In Greenock they queue outside Luigi's and in Kilmarnock it is Ferri's. And remember too Roberto's in Airdrie, Valerio's in Lanark and Crolla's of Galashiels. Often with petite Italian flags on their signs and menus, or shopfront livery of green, white and red, they are there. They are there in small town Scotland from its Highland tips to its lowland border, there ready to serve fish and chips as did their Nonnas and Nonnos before them.

Of course, Italian chippies are abundant in Scotland's cities too, but their presence in the provinces always strikes us outsiders harder. In towns, those greens and reds are bolder and there is a sharp element of surprise: 'How on earth did the Pacitti family end up in Auchtermuchty?', we might ask.

Once a hive of miners and shipbreakers, Bo'ness is a likeable if subdued town west of Edinburgh along the Firth of Forth. Where it isn't pleasantly confined by water it is surrounded by fields. In February 1940, three local men were walking among the wheat and barley when they spotted a pair of suspicious-looking figures. 'They appeared to be like foreigners,' said one of the locals, Robert Henderson, 'and when we gave chase they bolted and disappeared.' The West Lothian men soon caught their prey.

They had snared two German seamen, Auguste Friederich Hansstangel, 19, and Werner Heuer, 25, recently escaped from a nearby internment camp. The absconders were trying to reach Bo'ness and then Aberdeen, where they would stow away on a boat homewards. Henderson went to seek help and as the starving, emaciated Hansstangel and Heuer waited in the custody of the other two locals, a fish and chip van pulled up. 'Henderson's companions bought fish suppers,' reported *The Scotsman*, 'which their prisoners ate rapidly, with evident enjoyment.'

No van serves the area now but that hardly matters: Bo'ness has Corvi's, a charismatic, heritable chippy on Seaview Place. Antonio and Clementina Ferrari opened here in 1896; now, Corvi's is run by their great-great granddaughter, Mari-Ellena, and her husband Donnie. The act of sitting in Corvi's café area is to withdraw from normal time, a stopgap hour where the world outside may very well have disintegrated. Waiting unseen behind the dainty net curtains for your meal to arrive, you look to the 1960s frying range, still gorgeous and futuristic and resembling something from *The Jetsons*, and your brain floats elsewhere.

It was to Tuscany that mine travelled on the afternoon I visited. There is a hill town there named Barga where residents speak English with Scottish accents. Every August, they summon the long tables and celebrate La Sagra del Pesce e Patate – The Fish and Chip Festival. Strings of flags are suspended from roof to roof; il tricolore, of course, but also the Saltire. Skills first learned almost 150 years ago in Perth or Paisley and then handed down through the ages are used to deep fry now in the Tuscan summer. Some who gather served their time in Scotland and came home to live out their days in the sun. Others know only yarns of Scozia, having never visited but acquired their Scots-English from returned relatives.

As we glance to grey skies it is hard to conceive why anyone would trade the Tuscan hills for Britain. Yet the Italian existences those early emigrants vacated were drenched in hopeless poverty. They felt despair at a feudal, corrupt system which would not even offer them a basic education. This dejection fuelled an exodus that began in the last quarter of the nineteenth century and lasted for decades. Millions of Italians departed for the United States, Britain, Ireland and elsewhere in search of opportunity. Those who reached Scotland did not merely serve the fish and chip industry; they *were* the fish and chip industry.

Most Scots-Italians had their origins in Barga and the wider Lucca province, as well as a number of towns south of Rome. Some walked all the way to Britain. None spoke English. They were united not only by their nationality, but by an energetic work ethic and a flair for offering products that brought cheer to grim industrial streets. Many early arrivals to Scotland sold homemade ice cream and hot

drinks from carts, before graduating to permanent premises and serving fish and chips too. While their creations
sparked joy among natives, it is hard not to ponder quite
what a Tuscan farm hand must have made of central belt
Caledonia with its clanking ironworks and demonic
furnaces. The soft scent of lemon trees had given way to
acrid sulphur.

Italians were lured into the fish and chip trade by the
simplicity and cheapness of setting up shop. As de Gernier
had demonstrated in Dundee, little more was needed than a
preparation area for simple ingredients and a pan in which to
fry them. Not that such simplicity made for a pleasant existence: chip shop work meant long, grubby hours among rank
odours that seemed to meld into a fryer's skin and nest in
their hair. As they gutted and filleted haddock, and peeled
whole hillocks of spuds, hands used to the sun's balm now
solidified with aching cold.

Further perils of the trade came from the clenched fists of
others. Italians kept their chip shops open late, serving the
volatile post-pub herds. The slightest grievance could erupt
swiftly into violence – fryers learned how to look after themselves. Some of the aggression they faced was rooted in
xenophobia or anti-Catholicism. Most Scots-Italians were
well-acquainted with the unwanted nickname 'Dirty Tallies'
and other terms of abuse. It did not help that from 1920 they
were officially referred to as 'Aliens' after a government Act
of that name. It added to a sense of displacement and inner
turmoil familiar to millions of emigrants down the ages;

Italians felt foreign here in Scotland, but exiled and remote from their homeland.

Despite all of this, during the inter-war years Scotland's fish and chip Italians prospered. Their graft and creativity grew money. By the 1930s, there were more than 4,000 Italians here, dispersed throughout the country and running the vast majority of chippies. In Dundee, 9 out of 10 were Italian-run.

Immigration numbers slowed, however, as the 1930s progressed. Britain permitted fewer 'aliens' to live here, and in Italy fascist dictator Benito Mussolini resented the emptying of so many towns and villages. *Il Duce* made it harder for natives to leave. His regime infiltrated life in Scotland too. Some chip shop owners and their families supported the fascist movement. In Glasgow, that meant attending meetings and social gatherings at La Casa Del Fascio in salubrious Park Circle. Many arrivals, by contrast, were resolutely *anti*-fascist – indeed, fleeing Mussolini became another motivation for leaving Italy.

This friction was embodied when workers from two Glaswegian fish and chip shops, Sam Forte and Bruno Sereni, travelled to Spain and fought on opposing sides – fascist and republican respectively – of its civil war. Back in Scotland, a vast Aid for Spain movement aimed at helping the republican anti-fascist cause had sprung up. One of its campaigns sought to provide 'Fish and Chips for Spain'. Events across the continent were creeping towards the chip shop queue.

2.

ALIENS AT THE FRYING RANGE

Edinburgh, Glasgow and Largs

The man screwed up his face as if he had just walked through a spider's web. It was that kind of rain. He was trudging his way down Great Junction Street in Leith. I watched him through the window of Guido's, the nearest fish and chip restaurant to my house. On this narrow tenement road, others cowered in doorways to avoid being splashed sodden by passing vehicles. Watching the scene from the snug interior with my Angel Cut Haddock soon to be served offered a comforting feeling, akin to finding a secure space during a childhood game of hide and seek.

Guido's is a dapper, modern place of bare brick walls and olive-green banquette seating. It is how a fish and chip restaurant would look the morning after a makeover on a Channel 4 programme about failing hospitality venues. 'Tomorrow's fish are still in the sea' proclaim large neon words fixed to the brick, which upon reading fostered in me a sense of guilt: there they were one day, just minding their own business ...

There were several others also hiding from the downpour in this agreeable manner. One man slowly swung his fork across the plate's surface, rounding up snippets of fish with the ardent concentration of a curler sweeping the ice. A couple enjoyed speculating whether the haddock was actually cut by angels, and an out-of-breath woman in gym clothes pondered the takeaway menu as reward for her exercise. 'You've got to be good to yourself,' she said to the kindly man behind the counter.

Outside, messages from the past floating beside some of those Great Junction Street doorways. In scuffed and withered painted letters they whisper of 'W. Donaldson, Chimney Sweep' or 'Andrew Cook, Engraver'; people and businesses long faded away. Yet it was these same signs which framed events terrifying to Italians one summer night in 1940.

On 10 June of that year, seething mobs descended upon the chip shops of this very street. Their windows were pulverised, along with those of Italian-owned ice cream cafés and newsagent shops in the area. Glass smithereens strafed the pavement. When the looting began, potatoes were hurled outwards through empty frames. They rolled bumpily across the cobbles, skiddy now through the torrents of fatty oil that the attackers had poured out. Boxes of cigarettes and chocolate bars were also flung, and then gratefully received by some. Frying ranges were heaved to the ground.

As they rampaged, anti-Italian chants and howls of abuse competed with the petrified screams of the mothers and children who lived above their family shops. Most of the Italian men – their dads and husbands – had already been taken away right in front of them.

This impromptu aggression followed Benito Mussolini's declaration of war on Great Britain earlier in the day. Through that one act, Italians in this country had become instant enemies. Speaking of those very people, the new prime minister, Winston Churchill, had reacted to news of Italy's move from neutrality to support for Nazi Germany with the words: 'Collar the lot!'

Churchill and the government – and, it turned out, many among the British population – feared a 'Fifth Column' uprising of Italians in Britain. A long list of apparently active fascists existed. A number of them, no doubt, attended activities at Glasgow's Casa Del Fascio. The potential of an 'enemy within' could not be tolerated. It did not matter that many of those to be targeted had been born here, that some had served Britain in World War One, or that large numbers of them opposed Mussolini's regime, some of whom had already signed up for active service to fight fascism.

All Italian men in Britain aged 16 to 70 were to be arrested and interned. The women, children and elderly male relatives they left behind would also face restrictions. Those who lived near the sea were instructed to move a minimum of 20 miles inland to prevent them from assisting a coastal invasion. Train travel required a permit, curfews limited times when they could go outside and access to radios and maps was barred.

In the hours prior to the 10 June night-time rioting, men within the specified age range were removed by police officers. Throughout Scotland, some were taken from behind their chip shop counters and led away while still wearing their reeking frying clothes. Local bobbies who had the previous week been queuing for haddock and chips were now carting off the people they'd ordered them from. In London, some 700 Italians were detained 'without formalities' over a few days in June, according to one newspaper report. Across Glamorgan and in Cardiff, and reflecting Wales' status as another hotbed of Italian fish and chip shops, 230 were swiftly detained. In towns and cities all over the land, such was the anti-Italian backlash that some chippies and cafés raised signs in their windows relaying messages such as 'British Owned' and 'British Staff Here'.

Wherever arrests took place, riots followed. In Soho, there were reports of battles between Italians and Greeks. Thousands of Liverpudlians congregated and threw bricks at the windows of Italian businesses across their city. In Edinburgh, the most devastating actions were carried out in areas near Great Junction Street. Crowds of between 1,000 and 2,000 had gathered as, according to The Scotsman, 'anti-Italian feeling found vent in an orgy of window-breaking', and after the disturbances had entered a second night, 'At many of the premises not a single pane of glass remained ...

there was a wave of looting, and in some cases premises were completely cleared of stock before the police could intervene.'

Police intervention did lead to the arrest of some rioters – men like Frank Slaven, a soldier in uniform who had kicked through the window of Nicola Valentino's chip shop on Edinburgh's Royal Mile. According to a policeman giving evidence in court, his actions had been inspired by 'an exuberance of national zeal'. On a similar theme, Lord Provost Dollan of Glasgow commented, 'We are not going to tolerate hooliganism masquerading as patriotism.' As Dollan's statement hinted, anti-Italian actions were prevalent in the west of Scotland too. Down the River Clyde in Port Glasgow alone, 15 of 17 Italian businesses – many of them chip shops – had been wrecked.

Though gripped by understandable terror as first their menfolk were taken and then rabid hordes invaded, Italians did not merely quiver and flinch. In her outstanding study of Italians in Scotland during World War Two, *Experiencing War as the 'Enemy Other'*, Wendy Ugolini offers several accounts of defiance. As a child, John Costa was at home above his parents' fish and chip shop when the rioters came: 'I must admit – it's a funny thing to say for a child of nine years old – I was not all that frightened. I was very angry. In fact, all I wanted to do ... I wanted to have a gun. I'd have sorted them with a gun.'

Another chip-shop child, Isabella di Lena, recalled: 'They started yelling at me, "Get inside or I'll throw something at you." I was so angry I couldn't even feel any fear ... And I'm glaring at them, you know? Glaring back at them.'

In his book *Tales of the Savoy*, Joe Pieri, long-time fish and chip café owner, told of a fellow Italian fryer he knew of in Glasgow; Emma, from Barga. When a swarm of people began hurling abuse outside her shop in Port Dundas, she replied with a volley of her own: 'Fuck Mussolini. Fuck Hitler. Fuck you all. Don't you touch anything, you bastards. You would all eat shite if I fried it!' The crowd withdrew. Emma's chippy, said Pieri, remained open and prosperous throughout the war.

Many of those taken from their fish and chip shops, homes and other businesses did not get the chance to defend themselves, never mind return and prosper. When the S.S. *Arandora Star*, a cruise ship deployed to convey internees from Britain to Canada, was torpedoed by a German U-boat, 486 Italians drowned. The tragedy occurred just three weeks after the events of early June. Among the dead were fish and chip shop owners and workers – fathers and husbands last seen by children and wives as they were taken by the police. Among them was Silvestro D'Ambrosio, a fish and chip restaurant owner from Hamilton. At 68, Silvestro had lived in Britain for forty-two years and applied for naturalisation shortly prior to Italy's declaration of war. Three of his sons were already serving in the British Army; two more had recently registered.

Those spared the horrors of the *Arandora Star* faced internment camps in Britain, the Isle of Man, Canada and

Australia. Conditions were frequently abhorrent. After a year and a half, and over the months that followed, those deemed unthreatening to Britain were released. Soon, they were back at the frying range, sometimes serving the very people who had smashed up their shops.

Returning was not always simple. In the Fife town of Cupar, a released Italian internee had his licence application to open a fish and chip shop refused. At the council hearing, a local army general violently opposed the idea of permission being given – 'The proper place for an Italian,' he said, 'is between a wall and a bulldozer.' By 1949, the *Sunday Post* was reporting that many chip shop owners were selling up. 'In Glasgow alone,' they claimed, 'more than a dozen businesses are for sale every week. Most, say a Glasgow agent, are owned by Italians, who are drifting out of the country.'

Continued rationing of raw materials and a cooking oil shortage made the post-war years difficult for all fish and chip shops owners. Yet the Scots-Italians were resilient – and seemingly forgiving. Grafting away, they soon prospered in what is, overwhelmingly, a tale of immigrant success. That much is obvious in those names above the shop, from Guido's of Leith and beyond.

The following day, Caledonian clouds had finally drifted away. 'That's the rain off,' a neighbour said to me. She was employing Scottish phraseology that I am used to, and yet every time a Scot announces that the rain is either 'on' or

'off', I imagine God pulling a giant lever. In Glasgow the
skies had stopped sobbing too, although the cobbles and flagstones of Merchant City still shined with a damp, turned off
television screen sheen. Sometimes here, it feels as though
the streets just wake up wet.

Promising words are painted on a gable end wall off
London Road. On a white background, in dark red grand
and bold letters they announce 'Val D'Oro' – 'Golden Valley'.
The building they are stamped upon has cradled a fish and
chip café since 1875. It was known at first as The Swiss
Restaurant, owned by the Beltrami family; in 1938, the
Corvis took it over, and it has been Val D'Oro ever since.

That late morning, too many people failed to glance
upwards as they walked past the façade of Val D'Oro. Heads
down, fixated on mobile phones or earphones in and march-
ing as if under command, they passed it by, bats in an art
gallery. In doing so, they missed a marvel of a shopfront, a
picturesque wonder on the most unremarkable street. Had
they looked, those passersby would have encountered charismatic, showground poster maroon letters, meticulously
rendered in the 1940s, offering Teas, Coffees, Snacks, Ices.
Then beneath them, an illuminated sign – the first in
Glasgow, no less – from the following decade re-announcing
Val D'Oro Restaurant in italicised block lettering.

Those on autopilot failed to notice a lofty, broad-
shouldered figure. He was lifting hanging baskets of flowers
onto hooks either side of Val D'Oro's double-doors, preen-
ing the set. Here, in his immaculate white apron, was Enrico

Corvi. His family have been readying the shop like this on most mornings for eighty-five years.

Enrico, a handsome and sociable sort in his early sixties, was having a trying time. The delivery man was late with a consignment of cooking oil and one of the frying range pans had a fault. Son Gianluca arrived and joined in with setting up, tuning the ice cream machine and fetching equipment from the kitchen. Together in their turning of dials and clanking of apparatus, they awoke Val D'Oro for another day. Their chatter was studded with bickering and affection as that between close fathers and sons always is.

It is easy to imagine that it was just the same when the young Enrico and his brother Luigi worked here alongside their father, Peter, until he died from cancer in 1992. Peter Corvi had arrived in Glasgow from Bo'ness, his parents having migrated there from Tuscany in the twenties. Enrico and Luigi's mother, Anne-Marie, was born in Salerno and had arrived in Scotland after World War Two, importing her communist politics with her. When Peter's father took over the shop from the Beltramis, this area – Glasgow Cross – was known for its culture of violence and petty crime. In his first few days at the counter, a policeman told him Val D'Oro would not last a week. Hard toil, long hours and a devotion to fine raw ingredients – hand-cut potatoes, fresh fish from Aberdeen – proved that officer emphatically wrong.

The Corvi kids and grandkids were destined for life at the frying range, as was the case for most Italian children of the chip shop. Traditionally, family and business were bound together. This fixed fate did not mean education or culture were neglected. Enrico is a graduate of the University of Glasgow and London's Webber Douglas School of Dramatic Art. Luigi is a magnificent operatic tenor who trained at the Royal Conservatoire of Scotland and studied opera in Italy. Books and music were central to life at home; Renata Tebaldi records bellowed from Anne-Marie's radiogram.

Visits to Val D'Oro became famous for an accompaniment beyond salt and vinegar. In his sonorous, velvet tones Luigi would perform 'Nessun Dorma' while frying haddock or serenade tables of customers with arias as he served their smoked sausage suppers. There was, perhaps, in his voice an aching sadness at what might have been; although called to audition at Covent Garden, when Peter Corvi became ill Luigi felt it his duty to turn down the opportunity and instead keep Val D'Oro running. The frying range would remain Luigi's stage, Formica tables his auditorium.

For many years a striking picture hung from the front of the shop. Artist David Adam had painted a vivid crucifixion scene depicting Val D'Oro and Glasgow Cross life. Peter Corvi stood prominent, a coin in his hand, among regular customers and local figures, such as a well-known busker. It was a tribute to Peter and the sacrifices he – and the family – made in working extraordinarily long hours and helping downtrodden locals.

Often, customers would point to Peter and talk with great emotion about favours he'd done them or times he'd bought Christmas presents for their children. The work also represented the struggles of Italians in Scotland more generally and the way each new generation remained loyal to the chippy, neglecting any other ambitions. 'The family heritage must go on,' Luigi told a BBC reporter in 2011, 'You don't want to be a traitor to the tradition.' Gianluca is now the man in charge of how the shop appears. He removed the painting some months prior to my visit ahead of a deep clean of Val D'Oro and it will not be returning. 'You should've left it!' interjected Enrico, warmly, as his son spoke.

Luigi and Enrico began working here during their childhoods. 'I was seven or eight when I started,' said Enrico, peering over a frying range that once towered beyond him. He repeatedly apologised to me for the morning's stresses and strains and for the interior having seen fresher days. Yet I loved every element of it: the art deco arms of the seating booths; the beige tables they bookend; the mid-century flooring in faded planet Mars maroon and dying house plant green; and the gallery of photographs and clippings that camouflage the walls, transforming them into a museum of everything that matters here from family history to Juventus *Scudetto* wins.

A workman in a white hardhat and orange overalls arrived and ordered four fritter rolls with brown sauce. The frying pans stirred and then gargled musically. I was not entirely sure what a fritter was, so asked. Potato in batter came the answer. 'Ah, we'd call that a scallop,' I said. 'Isn't that a fish thing?' replied Gianluca. As the workman looked out of the window, the three of us further discussed regional variations.

'Pop' versus 'Juice' or 'Ginger'. 'Chip butty' versus a 'roll and chips'. A 'bag of chips' versus a 'poke'. I broached the subject of Scotland's savage lack of scraps. 'Never mind why we don't have them. Why on earth do youse eat them?!' contested Gianluca. Enrico was with me and agreed that a scrap butty sounded delightful.

There is, too, a grave divide within Scotland's central belt over 'chippy sauce', a concoction of brown sauce and vinegar found on every counter in Edinburgh shops but absent in the west. Those I live among can't conceive of chips bereft of this tart liquid. Glaswegians perish the thought. 'If I was in the east,' said Gianluca, 'I would *demand* salt only.'

Conversation meandered to the history of the shop, and to war. The Corvi June 1940 tale is a fascinating one. 'This was such a violent area back then,' said Enrico. 'We had two shops – this and one across the road – both my grandfather's. The police basically alerted him to stay hidden out of the way when they were making the arrests. So he wasn't interned. And my uncle was in the army.' The mention of violence is not exaggerated, although the Corvis held their own – that same grandfather deployed an axe-handle to fend off a gangster demanding protection money. Peter once used a vinegar bottle as a weapon against a thief and Luigi apprehended two abusive customers by sitting on them.

The gurgling of the fryers snapped us back to the present. A builder had popped by for an 11.50am sausage supper. These had been some of the hardest times in Val D'Oro history. 'It has been a total nightmare,' confessed Gianluca.

'The cost of ingredients has doubled. Electricity and gas have more than doubled.' This, of course, was the same precarious landscape that all chippies were navigating during the era of my travels. Val D'Oro was also less busy than previously. 'You need strength and enthusiasm to run this place,' said Enrico, 'that's the problem. When we're quiet like this it's hard. And we shouldn't be quiet. Maybe the shop is too old. I don't know what it is. I still think fish and chips have got the appeal. But young people like their kebabs, their spicy chicken.'

Many chippies endure by finding a niche. Here, the same interior that the owners would like to update attracts customers from outside Glasgow. 'You've got your regulars and you've also got a lot of tourists. We survive quite nicely on tourists,' added Gianluca. Within minutes, a German in his twenties popped by and ordered a fish supper with 'everything on it, lots of everything, and curry sauce too.' Next, a Frenchman arrived, took a seat and declared Val D'Oro 'a museum of life'.

As ever in the pursuit of cultural experiences, I ordered a Fritter Supper. When my plate landed, I wanted to adore what Enrico and Gianluca had made. I liked this place and I liked them. I was nervous, as if unwrapping a present from a relative with a record of inappropriate gift choices, feigned grateful expression at the ready. With one look at their shapely chips – curved like wood shavings – I knew that everything was going to be all right. The fritter was a cosy slab of contentment, a revelation. It could have warmed the hands of a statue. Happily, it turned out that a meal of double potato was not the culinary equivalent of that fashion faux pas, double denim. 'How were the chips?' asked Enrico. 'I'm still not sure about this oil we're using.' I assured him of their greatness, but he remained unconvinced. They were good, he felt, but not as good as *before*, that time we all increasingly yearn for: 'Oh when I was a kid, the chips were amazing,' he added.

As I ate, I listened to the pans rising and churning, a television on the wall replying to their conversation. At full-pelt they sounded like a monsoon on a marquee. Sometimes they fizzed suddenly and emphatically and it was as if a hippo had belly-flopped into a jacuzzi. Father and son talked as they cooked, always striving to make battered ambrosia: 'These need to be a bit crispier, Gian,' and 'That's floating too high, Dad.' There were no countdown electronics or yelping alarms signifying when items were ready. Perhaps they listened for the sound of the fryers changing, moving in subtle octaves. Luigi may have been absent, but the music played on.

One o'clock ticked near. Enrico switched on a speaker that percolated songs onto the street outside – first, Elvis yodelling *Something* by The Beatles. An old lady called in and asked, 'Do you do lentil soup?' The pair cheerfully directed her to somewhere that did. Then they provided pound coins for a man who had queued to request change for a fiver. 'Do you sell fag papers at all, Enrico?', enquired the next customer, a woman in her thirties. 'You do? Ah grand.' Val

D'Oro was a haven and somewhere to trust, a tiny society in a fractured city.

A man with an entourage of shopping bags thanked Enrico for his lunch: 'I've not been here for twenty years, this is my first time back, and it's not changed a bit. It tastes just as good too.' 'That's the problem,' said Enrico. 'It hasn't changed, but I have. We should've changed a lot of things, but we didn't. You need a lot of money to modernise,' he sighed.

'You're still here. That's the main thing,' said the man as he left and returned to the present.

In Fair Fortnight – the second half of July – Glaswegians swarmed west. By boat and rail, they were scarpering from exhaling chimneys and the factory hooter to Largs and other seaside towns. Through the industrial age, this route was their escape to the coast. This afternoon the ScotRail carriages were tranquil. 'Don't forget to take your belongings with you before you leave the train,' nagged an announcement prior to every station. 'Well, I can't take them with me *after* I've left the train, can I?' said a passenger as we approached Kilwinning. His wife looked as if she had heard him say this several times before.

We passed the railway junction that leads to Prestwick and I thought of Giovanni 'Johnny' Moscardini. In that town used to be the Lake Café, his fish and chip restaurant. Born in Falkirk to parents who had emigrated from Barga,

Moscardini joined the Italian army during World War One as a machine gunner. Having recovered from shrapnel wounds, he travelled to Barga and began to play for the local football team. Moscardini was a forward possessing a ferocious shot honed in the back closes of Scotland. Scouts from professional clubs swarmed to see him play. The Scots-Italian signed for Lucchese, then Pisa and Genoa. He even scored seven goals in nine games for the Italian national team.

Then came a choice: calcio or the chippy? The frying range won. A better living could be made in the Moscardini family cafés of Campbeltown and Prestwick. Right until he hung up his chip scoop in the 1960s, few locals knew they were being served their fritter suppers by an Italian international. Now, the sports stadium in Barga is named after him. It is there that La Sagra del Pesce e Patate is staged each August.

It was a friend from Dumfries via Barga, the writer Giancarlo Rinaldi, who first told me about Moscardini. The Rinaldi story is another typical – and typically vivid – Scots-Italian yarn. Giancarlo's grandparents ran fish and chip shops in Dumfries from after World War Two until the 1980s. His grandfather, Romeo, had been imprisoned during the conflict for refusing to fight for Britain. His grandmother's first husband, meanwhile, was drowned aboard the *Arandora Star*.

'My nonna,' he explained to me, 'was circumspect about her nationality. To her dying day she did not want to draw attention to being Italian. Her father, husband and little brother were all shipped off and interned in 1940 as "Enemy Aliens". After the war,' continued Giancarlo, 'I think Italians were keen to pick up where they left off and there wasn't too much resentment because so many were in trades where you had to get on with your customers if you wanted to make a living. Any grudges had to be kept below the surface. It is also true that many Scots realised that a lot of Italians had actually left Italy to get away from Mussolini and were far from sympathetic to his cause.'

Plus, the Rinaldis clearly understood their audience. 'I also remember,' Giancarlo chuckled, 'growing up, that my grandfather kept huge boxes of chocolates on the top shelf at his fish and chip shop – the Locaro Café – and I wondered who on earth bought them. It turned out that they were regularly sold late at night to slightly inebriated husbands who had forgotten an important anniversary or birthday and were trying to make it up to their irate other half. He sold plenty.'

By a pimply sea the train crept up on Largs. The very first building visible beyond the station wall was a fish and chip restaurant, The Blue Lagoon. A large ornamental gorilla dwelled on the pavement outside. The zoo theme continued with tall glass box windows which made families eating their meals look like exhibits. Across the road sat Gino's Fryer, 'Serving Largs Since 1982'. There is hardly a patch of this pretty town unreached by intoxicating chippy scents.

Down by the seafront is where you'll find The Moorings, a café at the foot of an apartment block. Resembling the bow of a misplaced cruise ship, it is built upon the site of an illustrious restaurant with the same name. Three storeys tall and boasting a 1,000-capacity dancefloor, it was once owned by one of Largs' two rival Italian families, the Castelvecchis. Their competitors were the Nardinis. Both originated in Barga, and both claimed to be the Ayrshire town's finest purveyors of all things deep fried or frozen.

With the sea charging towards town as if running from some unseen foe, I continued along the esplanade, passing ice cream booths and fish and chip huts. The sky's bluster slid metal chairs along the beach like empty ski lifts and threw hats from heads, a slapstick poltergeist. An old couple watched a small fleet of amusement rides, she bobbing both shoulders along to the fairground music, he feeding her chips from a box. It was almost possible to see time rewind in front of them.

Behind this compelling scene hovered Nardini's café, an art deco alabaster palace of the good things in life. It has been here for almost ninety years, surviving World War Two despite Nardini men being interned on the Isle of Man. During its early life, Nardini's was the largest café-restaurant in Britain. It is a building fondly lodged in the memories of most who visit. First the sleek poise of the exterior transfixes, then the ship's ballroom glamour of the interior instils a feeling of awe and occasion, like that of a first visit to the circus.

Nardini's entry room is the ice cream parlour. Its leaning towers of cones and vessels of blazing flavours snatched my eyes upon arrival. Then, blissful sounds hauled me into the main dining area: the clinks of cutlery on plates; a service bell I wanted to run towards like a monk late for prayers; chirpings of chitchat rising and falling and fulsome laughter striking the chandeliers.

From my table I looked upwards to the walls and ceilings with their art deco flourishes and across to the stage with its sleeping piano. Nardini's, it now seemed obvious, was a venue and not a restaurant, and going there was to attend an event or indulge in a pastime. It had the democratic span that the best places do. A middle-aged man on his own held his fork like a spear and stabbed at his haddock as if he thought it might at any moment hop through the window and back into the ocean. Young couples took nervous blobs of ice cream from glasses apparently modelled on the Olympic Torch. Husband and wife pensioners sat fully contented in the silences between their words. On larger tables, three or even four generations were gathered, grown up grandchildren privileged to be hearing Nana's stories all over again. I found it hard to imagine many other cuisines that could bring so many ages together.

Then, an oval plate landed before me and I could look at nothing else: haddock the shape of a Viking longboat, its batter a shade of copper, with a herd of fluffy chips. Being here now seemed a fine stroke of fortune.

Opposite my table, the husband pensioner headed for the Gents, which prompted his wife to reapply her lipstick. He returned, they smiled at one another and then departed. It was time for me to do the same. Thanking Italy, I left for Lancashire.

3.

RAG 'N' BARM MAN

Blackpool

As our train fell still at Blackpool North station, a woman calmly announced: 'Oh. Blackpool? I meant to go to Liverpool.' This relaxed tone suggested that she was regularly beset by such happenings. It is a nice way to live, I suppose.

The future was being written by cranes here. 'Making Blackpool Better' boasted the slogan on wooden screens masking building sites. 'Thank you for your patience as we improve your town.' As is so often the case in seaside places, here in the shadowy streets behind the waterfront a certain sadness lingered. Lost souls loitered in twos and threes, occasionally asking for help but mostly struggling on in their own abandoned mini-society. Struck by substance abuse and exiled to coastal rooms, they do not make the front of postcards. A woman tipped coins into a BT payphone. When was the last time you used a payphone? They're a thing of romance to the lucky among us – secretive teenage calls to a girl in another village, saying 'I love you' before the pips. But there is at the seaside so often a friction between candy floss glee and the blight of addiction.

Most of us train passengers scarpered for the seafront and its amusement arcades, slotting our own coins in machines. Urged downhill by tram tracks, I passed a cabaret bar promising a refreshingly precise Seven Acts Per Night. Then came the ornate grandeur of the Winter Gardens concert halls, and finally the promenade where the first thing I noticed was North Pier Fish and Chips. Outside, a lone motorcyclist used his last chip to stub out a dewdrop of vinegar, helmet balanced across the table in place of company. It is sometimes difficult being alone at the seaside, a place more for couples new and old, or families. A few minutes later, opposite Blackpool Tower, a young woman approached me and said: 'You look like the kind of man who'd know: What time's the next vintage tram?'

Beneath a sharp blue sky the Irish Sea marched outwards. Optimists in shorts lugged fold-up chairs across the sand. 'Eeeee, it could be Tenerife,' said a man in a Halifax Town shirt, 'if it weren't for the smell of donkey shite.' I looked along the sands and towards Southport. Britain's oldest man, John Tinniswood, born in 1912, resides in a care home there. Tinniswood has repeatedly cited one particular meal as central to his longevity: fish and chips, every Friday. 'Looking forward to my next visit to the chippy has kept me young,' he told the *Mirror* in 2019.

'Prom Chippy. Open Now' declared an A-board beside the resolutely shuttered Prom Chippy. Other establishments spoke for themselves – arcades with their machines' chirpy muttering, trilling bingo callers ('Flirty one, 31. Right any way up, six and nine, 69'), or the boasts of wall-mounted loudhailers affixed to attractions. 'We let you see, hear, touch, smell and feel,' said one. 'It's hilarious fun, and it's sometimes a bit scary.' A bit like life, I reflected. Nearby was the den of Gypsy Petulengro, a fortune teller whose signage confessed that she had been 'Patronised by Royalty'.

It was the flurry of chippies that kidnapped my gaze, though. There was Papa's and Harry Ramsden's, The Frying Squad and Big Fish Trading, Blackpool Fish Factory and Sillock's, each tantalising scent causing me to salivate as I passed. Now I had to undertake the arduous task of selecting one to dine from.

During childhood trips to the seaside, my family would shun the gaudy offerings of seafront chippies. The best places, apparently, were to be found in the yards and ginnels removed from the ocean. This was where the *locals* feasted, a mysterious unseen breed of batter sages. That these shops were cheaper than those nearer the beach was merely coincidence. Such principles cannot be easily shed, and so it was that I opted for Lily's Traditional Fish and Chips, one street shy of the esplanade's blinking lights and luminous rock shops.

Lily's didn't need the flashy front. It had a reserved glow of its own. Here was a tulip cut from the garden rather than an expensive bouquet. With immaculately symmetrical tables presenting identically placed condiment bottles, walls decorated in serene shades of blue and a display shelf of model boats and lighthouses, it had the relaxed but efficient aura of a canteen for retired sailors afflicted by OCD.

Sadly, there were no scraggly-bearded men with wise eyes warbling sea shanties. Instead, Greatest Hits Radio went to war with the frying ranges and their bubbling symphony. At the counter, the man taking my order offered a smile so friendly that I presumed it was for somebody stood behind me. He was framed by two colossal jars of pickled eggs and onions so that he resembled a hook-a-duck stall proprietor behind bowls of prize goldfish. It struck me that being in a fish and chip shop *should*, for a few minutes at least, give the childish rush of visiting a fairground or the anticipation of awaiting a few pound coins at the end of a grandparent's visit.

In those minutes of waiting while my meal danced around the cauldrons, I read through the menu. Here in Lancashire, the butty is absent and the roll expelled: listed in the Side Orders were 'Chip Barm £3.60' and 'Barm Cake 80p'. Also listed was 'Gravy Curry Beans Peas 95p', and I hoped the lack of separating grammatical marks was intentional. Imagine all those slushy delights fraternising on one plate, as if Jackson Pollock had been commissioned to portray the north. It would take one hefty barm cake to mop that up.

After the opening shift at Val D'Oro and the lunchtime commotion of Nardini's, I had reached Lily's during the mid-afternoon slump. In this No Man's Land between meals, frying staff recuperate while refreshing their shops for the teatime onslaught. The queue of an hour ago seems impossible, a hologram. The temperature thins and drops from that of a glasshouse to a shady patio. The gap is a truce, an armistice of the frying pans, only now fired for each individual order. Customers are sparse, like open shops on a 1950s Sunday. Alongside me at 3pm in Lily's, there were only two couples: one in their forties arguing about his excessive mobile phone use; and another whose north-eastern male half liked to end most sentences with the words 'Well, I had nowt better to do.' A few others bobbed in for takeaways. 'I don't feel right today,' said one old lady. 'Large cod and chips'll shift it, please, flower.'

Then, from amidst the lull, a plate landed in front of me. Its chips were the bewitching colour of cartoon doubloons. In hunks they huddled, resembling a beavers' dam. The cod was strident – proud with tips that pointed like dunce caps. It wore batter ridges in sound wave formations. A slice of lemon balanced upon one end of the fish as if it were a seal preparing to bounce a ball, and on its midriff a sprig of seasoning offered fig-leaf modesty.

In one bite I was there again, remembering what a fried fish tasted – *felt* – like on those cold evenings sitting on the village chippy wall. This sizzled cod became a bolt of fork lightning with one prong in the present and another in the past. Back-street Lily's was already an exquisite time machine, and I hadn't even started on the chips yet.

* * *

'We are concerned about the tolerance of the fish and chip van,' wrote the chairperson of Corbridge Business and Visitor Network to her fellow members in early 2005. 'What next? Caravans? Gipsies? Car boot sales?' She railed at how 'photographic evidence' proved that 90 per cent of the van's customers lived in council houses. With its visibly proletarian patrons – what *were* they wearing in these photos? Mining helmets? Clogs? – a mobile chippy in the prosperous Northumbrian town clearly represented some sort of lardy apocalypse.

Northumbrian disdain echoed that unleashed in Frinton-on-Sea, Essex, during the early 1990s. The Edwardian resort had until then avoided monstrous seaside enclaves such as amusement arcades, funfair rides and pubs. Then a man named Ernie White opened its first chippy, The Nice Fish and Chip Shop. White eluded the town's fussy permit rules by buying an existing café, The Copper Kettle, and installing fryers. A very English brand of hell broke loose.

'They call me a yob and tell me to get back to Walton-on-the-Naze, where I come from,' he told *The Times*, 'but we're here to stay.' Vox pops with locals corroborated White's words. 'Will I use the place?' said one man. 'Not likely. Ghastly fried fish, wouldn't touch it.' A dog-walking woman added, 'It's the smell I can't stand. It will drift across town, travel for miles and get into everyone's clothes.'

Yet queues amassed outside The Nice Fish and Chip Shop, which had now splintered Frinton into factions. 'It's about time we had one of these in Frinton,' concluded one customer, 'It's ridiculous that a few toffee-noses and their friends on the council can stop people eating what they want for the best part of 80 years.'

The Frinton dog-walker's aromatic complaints – hard to comprehend for those of us seduced by a chippy's vapours – had been heard before. In 1957, the local council granted permission for Eton's first fish and chip shop. Then, fellow high street businesses forced a reversal of the decision – deep-fried fumes would impregnate the pages of their antiquarian books and infest their plush garments. That 300 residents had signed a petition in support of the chippy did not matter; Eton could not be disfigured in this manner, and the idea of its schoolboys flocking to the frying range was a cause of panic.

There had been a strain of sneering towards fish and chip shops since their 'Frying Tonight' signs were first hoisted in the Victorian era. Scorn based on the stenches they belched forth was often justified. For the first decades of the industry's existence, most chippies absolutely stank. Untreated oils and tallow fats melded with raw fish and loitered heavily in a shop's unfiltered atmosphere. These emissions escaped through doors and windows, becoming a neighbourhood nuisance. Not even vinegar could suffocate them.

An 1891 court case about an apparently noxious fish and chip shop in Middlesbrough embodied the problem. Thomas Hatfield had opened a chippy on Borough Road to the immediate displeasure of his next-door neighbour, John Bow. In front of judge and jury, Bow's solicitors argued that the shop should be closed and their client entitled to compensation. Hatfield's establishment, they argued, had exhaled effluvia, causing illness and forcing the Bows to leave their home. Their medical experts compared the stench to 'rancid candles' and claimed it left them feeling nauseous. Hatfield responded by highlighting the fine health of his resident sixteen children, and a recital of one of the poems he had scratched into the shop's window entertained the court ('Here, fish and potatoes as fine as can be / So come for your supper and do without tea'). The jury found for Bow.

The case mattered to the wider culture of fish and chips because it centred on a philosophical and legal question: could the trade be defined as a 'nuisance'? In the years that followed, similar legal actions were taken and health officials linked the eating of fish and chips to illnesses such as enteric fever. In 1910 Dr Trotter, a medical officer in County Durham, reported how 'Cases approaching ptomaine poisoning were constantly cropping up. Where beef dripping was used no harmful effects occurred, but the grease, and tallow admixtures frequently employed in cooking caused evil results.' Concerns meant that during the Edwardian era the industry was legally reclassified as an Offensive Trade.

Pesky odours and hygiene hysteria were not the only causes of animosity towards the fish and chip industry. Snobbery, most of it drenched in class prejudice, fuelled derision. To the middle and upper classes, this was the food of the poor, its outlets seedy lairs of filth and even immorality.

There is a clear and snooty attitudinal line from prim Victorians perturbed by the rise of the workers' dish to complainants in Corbridge, Frinton and elsewhere. Not that chippy customers saw it that way – they, after all, had discovered and appreciated the magnificence of a food that would one day become a symbol of national identity years before the moneyed classes did. Even if that discovery came from economic necessity, fish and chips were still *theirs*. They laughed along to music hall routines set in the chip shop queue and then ate chips in the open air on the way home.

A December 1941 edition of *The Broons* comic strip typified working-class ownership of a chippy tea in fictional form. A middle-class guest, Mrs Fitzgerald, is visiting the family home. Maw Broon cannot fathom what to feed her – fish and chips are suggested but the women of the house agree that their guest is too posh for such a thing. 'Hoo could we no' hae fish an' chips the nicht – whit's wrang wi' them?' moans Granpaw Broon. 'Whit's better than walkin' hame on a cauld nicht eatin' chips oot o' a warm bag?' One of the twin boys agrees: 'Jings! It's awfy haein' tae be posh. There's far mair fun bein' common!' At the strip's end, to the astonishment of all Broons, Mrs Fitzgerald walks in with a parcel of fish and chips – 'A surprise for you.' For one teatime at least, unity across social classes breaks out from among the newspaper wrapping. Whether Mrs Fitzgerald tries a Pea Buster is unclear.

During and after World War Two, as the Broons storyline hinted, fish and chips became more widely accepted, and even revered, right across British society. However, haughtiness lingered. Four years after the conflict, a Canon T.H. Tardrew addressed York Minster. Further war could be prevented, he said, by increased education. However, a study of 'the faces of those who compose the queues waiting for … the dispensing of fish and chips' had left him to conclude that 'the future, if dependent on intelligence, is rather bleak'. By 1987, condescension of chip shop customers had passed from the pulpit to the podium as Junior Health Minister Edwina Currie launched an odd broadside against northern nurses who smoked and ate fish and chips. Interestingly, she victimised Blackpool residents in particular, claiming that 'People round here are taking hearty breakfasts, eating fish and chips several times a week, and perhaps drinking a little too heavily.' This was the era of individualist Thatcherite escape from class traditions and leaving that chippy queue behind for more ambitious sustenance. As AA Gill wrote a few years later, 'Fish and chips were, well, something to aspire out of.'

In 2014, a *Daily Telegraph* article claimed that fish and chips were 'No longer the working man's nourishment' and now 'classless'. Theirs was a country in which snobbery had given way to patriotic pride. The meal and its purveyors were now key symbols of shared British identity, and people the world over knew these isles for their battered cod.

One motivation for my dot-to-dot chippy tour was to test the reality of this, or at least eat well while trying. I had come to Blackpool because it was the seaside, yes, but also because it remains a working-class resort. Like fish and chips, this place is also accustomed to snobbery. Perhaps there is an association there – a town crammed with chippies is one to be sneered at. This is epitomised in a line often deployed in media features down the years – that there is 'More to' Blackpool or Scarborough or Southend 'than just fish and chips'.

There was a further reason for coming to Blackpool: the aforementioned density of chippies. It is hard to imagine any settlement possessing more chip shops per head of population than here. To those of us transfixed by the sorcery of mushy peas and wooden forks, this Lancastrian town is Shangri-La with scraps on top.

For more than a century, people have been arriving here and spending at least some of their day perusing fish and chip shops. Edwardian millworkers tipped out of charabancs or spilled from trains and then selected a chippy queue to join. That they consumed this same meal in their home-towns of Bolton or Wigan did not matter. Here, *they* – not the factory hooter – decided when it was time to eat. Further, this was an elevated form of fish and chips; local cod from Fleetwood along the shore, scoffed next to the lashing Irish Sea. Most of us agree that, somehow, fish and chips taste better when consumed on the coast. This could be for culinary reasons – in theory, if not always in practice, we are eating fresher fish caught by local boats. Or, perhaps deep down we perceive that people who live nearest the ocean, and whose families have often survived by its produce, know how best to prepare and cook its harvest. I suspect, though, that fish and chips taste better at the seaside because when we are there we are living a day out or a holiday. This happy association and freedom from humdrum, regular existence enhances their appeal and taste.

Next for those jolly holidaymakers and coach day trippers, there is intense concentration in picking where to eat. Some visitors are fortunate: they have a regular, a local far from home, a fixed destination that has never let them down. 'We always go there,' they say, a catchphrase alongside other seaside classics such as 'It'll burn off, that' and 'I could definitely live here, me.' For many, though, there is now an inspection period in which they amble between shopfronts, slowing to assess queue and condiment situations, then bickering about one another's fussiness in between outlets. They resemble those locals you see out for a passeggiata, an evening stroll, when holidaying in a continental town. Only they are more prone to be saying things like 'She charged me 50p for a ketchup sachet in there last year. And she keeps the wooden forks behind the counter,' or 'He leaves the skin on his fish, him. It's not right.'

Suddenly, they will settle on somewhere, often because it is cheap or clean – or cheap *and* clean. Usually, however, it will have been a particular scent that guided them to a choice almost subconsciously. Just as people prefer certain perfumes or aftershaves, so they have a weakness for one fish and chip shop's aromas over another's. Comic strip vapour trails navigate them inside. Noses are victorious over eyes. Perhaps a familiar brand of frying oil bestows an unrivalled sense of coming home. Or maybe one scent immediately transports the searching diner to a happier, younger time.

While walking off my Lily's lunch I decided to recreate this selection parade, embarking on a late afternoon observational chippy crawl from one end of Blackpool to the other. Some people trek around South America and some tour the great art galleries of Europe. I share their need for intrepid discovery and cultural enrichment, and so my own voyage began at Sam's Chippy on Dickson Road, Blackpool.

Perky white lettering on a red background announced Sam's, below which were listed some of its offerings – 'Fish. Pies. Sausages. Puddings. Colddrinks.' That the latter was all one word and appeared at the sign's extreme reminded me of drawing posters as a child and having to cram in the last few words in a headline due to artistic miscalculation. I was pleased to encounter the word 'Puddings', which in a Lancastrian chippy context has nothing to do with desserts, referring instead to steam-cooked suet pies, or rag puddings. I'd say the two dishes were similar were I not at risk of being lynched by a vigilante mob from Oldham or Bury. Such are the wild passions and vagaries of local chip shop variations and terminology. From beyond a turret of mushy pea tubs, a young server glanced over and so I moved on. An explorer must not disturb his subjects any more than is necessary.

Ten doors along dozed Finesse Fish & Chips, resting until evening service. With a hand to my forehead like brave

Captain Birdseye scanning the horizon, I pressed against its window and peered inside. An electric blue fly zapper remained vigilant on the wall. Finesse had the tallest counter I had witnessed in quite some time. Smaller customers must appear bodyless, floating Yoricks requesting curry sauce. Its height shipped me backwards to boyhood, and the blind anticipation of unseen chip shop voices as my parents ordered. Soon after Finesse came The Catch, a corner chip shop in magpie shades. The falling sun caught suddenly against its chrome frying ranges and reflected back across the road in my direction. I feared sudden combustion as with an ant beneath some rascal child's magnifying glass, so fled.

Topping Street offered Yorkshire Fisheries. A bold label indeed in this county, it may as well be called 'Come and Have a Go If You Think You're Hard Enough Fisheries.' Despite this provocative approach to naming, a reserved font of the breed usually deployed by funeral directors hinted at the regal status of this place, as did its pale gold and emerald frontage. There has been a fish and chip shop here since 1907, so perhaps fervent Lancastrian patriots do not smash in its windows because that would be a bit like punching a kid with glasses.

Nearby, I encountered Tower Fisheries, the first 'i' in that second word replaced with a graphic of Blackpool Tower. It sold 'Yorkshire Fishcakes' and I began to wonder if Topping Street was some kind of White Rose enclave. Any minute now, Geoffrey Boycott and Alan Titchmarsh would appear arm-in-arm singing 'On Ilkley Moor Bar t'At' and I'd have to run into the sea for escape. A woman in a fleece jacket featuring a large illustration of a wolf left the shop, smiling and swinging her thin 'Enjoy Delicious Fish & Chips' plastic bag through the air. Chippy night restores in us the glee of leaving a sweetshop following a pocket money raid.

Around the corner, a man wearing a long black coat and fedora hat, and clutching a battered old briefcase, read a menu in the window of The Sea restaurant before shuffling away, perhaps to 1935. The Sea is a sharp, modern venue possibly for those breezy, saintly occasions when a family decide to 'go posh' for Nana's birthday. Empty now, I glanced inside and could imagine the faint outlines and electric currents of people celebrating.

The clacking of a chip scoop drew my attention to the Cleveland Chippy. Outside, a man clasped a bag of chips in one hand while taking a phone call with the other. He looked longingly and helplessly at the steaming package and I thought he was about to plunge his face into it, even before a circling seagull could. On streets wrinkled with veteran bed and breakfasts I envisaged old-fashioned landladies and their laminated 'No Fish n Chips in Room' signs. One, Mount Mellory, towered directly over a chippy, the Mickey Finn, and offered rooms for £10 per night. A Mount Mellory staff member balanced on a roof ledge three storeys high, replacing a tile. Two blasts of a car's horn below in the street startled him perilously. 'Fucking dickhead!' he cried.

Across from Micky Finn's roosted the Palma Café, a striking 1960s establishment painted in traffic cone orange. On each table, small open caskets held condiments as if awaiting customers to lean in and pay their respects. Trays loitered in stacks, ready to be shunted across metal rails. This, after all and as declared by outside signage, was a 'Self Service Cafeteria'. If Glasgow's Val D'Oro resembled an exhibit exuding post-war optimism; here was the next room in the museum – a 1960s haven in which the future had just about arrived.

Finn's and the Palma were a gateway to Central Drive, something of a chippy corridor. This was the densest terrain of my hike so far. The two were neighboured by Meat 'N' Plaice, which offered an intriguing dish named 'Adult Popcorn and Chips'; TT Fish & Chips; and the adamantly red and white Stevonia, established in 1919 and wearing window awnings that brought to mind a cuckoo clock. I waited for the hour mark but regrettably no ornate model haddocks emerged from the windows beneath.

Some yards on and roaming now towards the sea, I locked eyes on a specimen called simply 'Fish & Chips'. It felt a bold move, avant-garde almost, to opt for such a name. Fish & Chips had a minimalist, spartan look now often strived for by interior designers but achieved here by making absolutely no changes in perhaps half a century. Stencilled black letters on a white window board advertised its restrained menu and distinctly retro prices – fish £4.50, pies £1.80, potato scallops 50p. Once again, Blackpool was proving time travel possible.

On Chapel Street I paused to observe the swatted-hornet coloured signage of Waverley Café, 'Est 1935' and bragging that 'Our Fresh Fish is Skinless and Boneless.' A young female server looked vacantly outwards, probably dreaming of elsewhere, or dreaming at least of working somewhere that didn't serve such ancient culinary artefacts as Lamb's Liver and Onions. Next door in another branch of The Sea, families gorged and giggled, a teenager tottered from foot to foot whilst restlessly awaiting his order and a man leaned across the table to snare one of his partner's chips with a wooden fork. Outside, a pensioner chatted with her dog and referred to a sign across the road. '"Blackpool's Only Heated Dog Café",' she read. 'I didn't even know there were any *un*heated ones.' The dog failed to reply, possibly hypnotised by chip shop aromas.

My expedition progressed to the promenade, a territory rendered precarious by the menace of mobility scooters. Here, one lapse in concentration might result in violent contact with a pensioner from Ormskirk. Vigilance was essential. Rejoicing in the vivid shades and jaunty racket of rock shops and bingo houses was an existential risk. To become lost in the euphoria of a boundless blue sky and luscious ocean was to dice with death.

Illustrating this motorised anarchy, a kamikaze OAP raced towards the descending electronic shutter of Ocean Basket Fish & Chips. The frantic dash brought to mind Indiana Jones scurrying towards caved shelter during a landslide. The woman was too late, and instead made for Captain's Table Family Fish & Chips, a restaurant inside an amusement arcade. I hoped that there was crossover between the two and, for example, customers could attempt to win their own battered sausages on a grabber machine.

Behind the prised-open doors of Food2Go, a couple snuggled and shared a tray of chips. The romantic ambience was undermined by the shop's Tannoy speakers. Tuned to a local radio station, they now blasted out news of a double stabbing in nearby Blackburn. Between Central and South piers flowed chippies galore. There was CFresh, 'Voted Blackpool's Best Licensed Chippy', and Salt & Vinegar, where a toddler napped in a buggy as his mum spent precious free time with a cardboard trove of fried treasure. Then came The Cod Father, its lone customer a workman wearing orange overalls queueing for his end-of-shift reward, Mother Hubbard's where a jovial man with a retirement tan rubbed his hands together and said 'Just smell that' before entering, and another restaurant called Fish & Chips. Its logo depicted a cod sporting a chef's hat and holding a chip in one of its fins, apparently oblivious to its own fate. Nearby, the wall of Romany Lavinia Clairvoyant posed the question, 'Will you spend your days with your husband or lover?' and reassured passers-by that 'Her knowledge is not from books.'

Then came a melancholy discovery – the cosy corner premises of Traditional Fish & Chips with an announcement swiped into its grimy windows: 'Sorry Shut.' It was accompanied by a dusty sketch of a frowning face. Seats were hoisted onto tables in the manner of a classroom during the school holidays and the fryers had fallen silent. After the blinking lights and seething pans of so many living concerns, here came a reminder that these were gruelling times to try and run a chippy. 'Today I will be happier than a seagull with a stolen chip,' declared the sign above a café opposite.

I roamed onwards past Pablo's, with its interactive ordering screens, and Fish Ahoy, another shop to boast 'Traditional' fish and chips. That word's frequent use – and ditto the deployment of 'Proper' fish and chips – in this trade demonstrates what we customers need the dish to be: unchanging, trustworthy, habitual, never revamped. A visit to the chippy must be consistent and offer no surprises. Should some rogue fryer meddle by announcing 'Thrice-cooked chips', or that he now cooks in truffle oil, Albion would shake.

Towards the Pleasure Beach yet more specimens hovered into view. At Orange Fish, a staff member polished windows ferociously as if doing so might ward off the threat of ever having to use the dreaded words 'Sorry Shut.' There was a sign advertising that their fish and chips were Halal, something repeated in a number of windows here. It reflected another chapter of this dish's rich immigration story: that many families of Middle Eastern and South Asian origin, both Muslim and non-Muslim, operate – and eat from – chippies. The Beachcomber offered fish and chips 'From £2.99', a throwback price echoed by a cherished throwback remark that an old lady made to me as she moved aside from Joe's Cut Price Rock stand: 'Eee, I make a better door than a window, don't I love?'

Now the sun was drooping towards the Irish Sea and Blackpool had run out of fish and chip shops for me to ogle.

That each one of the thirty or so I'd seen on this golden safari was different to the next made me quietly elated. Here were tiny republics in a homogenised world of chain stores and eateries. They dazzled in their individuality and idiosyncrasies, a vibrant miscellany. Imagine sneering at that.

4.

PANDA POPS UNDER THE STARS

Oldham and Mossley

When it was Mr Barlow's turn to take us swimming, there could only be one post-baths source of sustenance. The gaudy automation of the vending machine or a milkshake from the leisure centre café were not even worth contemplating. Using his industrialised arms as temporary barriers, he would stop his son, Richard, and me as the three of us walked alongside each other through the car park. Then, turning to face us, he'd declare in an Oldham accent thicker than lard: 'Let's get fish 'n' chips. And we'll eat them outside, like they're supposed to be eaten.'

Mr Barlow emphasised the word 'outside', elongating it so that it seemed to grow more syllables and stretch above our heads. His line was always delivered freshly and with endearing enthusiasm despite fortnightly repetition. I used to wonder who had decreed that this was how fish and chips should be consumed and if there was an actual law. Richard suspected his dad didn't want his Vauxhall Cavalier to honk of cod and vinegar; we were both 11 or 12, on the cusp of a more cynical age.

On these dim midweek evenings in the old coal town of Selby, Abbey Fisheries would gleam like a gold tooth in a barren mouth. It seemed impossibly decadent for a school night. Mr Barlow might as well have announced that we were going to the casino. Seen close up as we queued, a mist of condensation veiled the shop window, adding to its contraband allure. Bleary ghosts bobbed around inside, later revealed to be the women who worked behind the counter. But no cloud could obstruct the seductive aroma that glided from the shop each time the door was opened, nor the melodic refrain of a chip lifter tinkling against the range, each movement one small scoop towards our turn. Inside, we awaited the heavenly call of 'Who's next please?', a sound even sweeter than a fire alarm during double chemistry. The vending machine had nothing on this.

Mr Barlow took our orders and then relayed them to a server. This was the nervous moment when we boys worried that through Chinese Whisper-style distortions, our requests of battered sausages and chips with Bubblegum Panda Pops might become something else. There was a risk that any such adjustments might be wilful since Richard's dad considered anything other than cod or, at a push, haddock to be harbingers of moral decrepitude. Not for him a liquid accompaniment: 'I'll just make a brew when we get home,' he'd say.

'Do you want these open or wrapped, flower?' a ghost would ask. 'Oh open, love,' Mr Barlow merrily chimed. 'We're gonna eat them outside, like they're supposed to be eaten.' Behind his back, Richard and I mouthed those words in synchronicity. A salt and vinegar monsoon later and there we were back on the street, only this time with paper bales of the good stuff. Chip heat reanimated our cold and chlorine-crimped fingers. Batter flew smoke signals into the dank evening, steam-drying our uncombed and sodden hair. We ambled cautiously onwards, eating ravenously but guarding our packages. It was as if we were following a star while carrying simmering gifts.

Eating outside extinguished etiquette. Under the sky, we could talk with our mouths full and pincer our food with eager fingers. Wooden forks were plunged into a plump chip and left dormant, tiny Excalibur swords welded into Maris Pipers. There would be no pots to wash, either. After a while, we'd find a wall to roost upon, now rinsing our waxy mouths with Panda Pops. Everything felt slow and tranquil, especially compared to our other dining arenas of the boisterous school dinner hall and the family table with its sibling squabbles. Then, our papers would be bare or our stomachs too packed for more chips and suddenly the evening was cold again. It was time to scrunch what was once treasure into trash.

Although we gently ridiculed him, as children should do to repetitive dads, there was ample substance to Mr Barlow's sentiments. Eating a chippy tea al fresco – and had we known

and used that phrase, he would've winked and then replied
'Al Fresco? Is that the Italian lad United've signed?' – was and
is a gladdening pursuit. Under nature's roof happy times are
lived. There is the arm-in-arm bag of chips shared after a
cinema date, the ravenously gorged fish supper after five too
many pints and the family beach picnic with Grandma and
her walking stick guarding against seagull raids. Not far away,
other seaside visitors will be eating their meals eyes-down
from trays unrolled on their laps like resting pilgrims consult-
ing their holy books.

Besides pronouncing the supremacy of outside eating, Mr
Barlow also offered a further truth apparently indisputable to
him. In between our scoffing sounds and tittle-tattle came
another frequently reprised line: 'Fish and chips were
invented in Oldham, y'know. No wonder I like them.' Thirty
years on, I decided to investigate his claim.

The tram harrumphed its way free of Mancunian suburbs
and pushed up into the old cotton-spinning parishes of east
Lancashire. In Chadderton and Nimble Nook, huge old mills
lingered, titans from a faded age with their proud names
yelled in brick, RAVEN or NILE. These mansions of graft
were closely aligned with another Victorian industry: the fish
and chip trade. Some early chippies fried in cotton seed oil,
an offshoot of mill production. Then, fish and chip shops
spread wildly owing to millworker demand. As women – and
children – were recruited into gruelling toil, time for meal

preparation vanished. The idea of menfolk helping remained preposterous to husbands, and so this cheap, filling meal became a mainstay in Pennine mill territory. Out from the tyranny of the dusty, deafening workshop they emerged and into homespun chippies on redbrick terrace street corners. Chippy night was not an occasional, yearned-for parental proclamation; it was a necessity on several evenings every week.

Stepping out from the Metrolink carriage at Oldham Central, I felt the mild vertigo encountered when standing on a table. The tram had hoisted us far above Manchester and now the sky seemed closer. It was a clear denim blue and yet biting pellets of rain flicked ears and pocked skulls. On Clegg Street, a man almost gouged out one of my eyes with his abundant umbrella, an unknowing sentry protecting the citadel from intruders like me. All around, locals walked in a stooped fashion as if trying to duck the raindrops. I imagined those mill women, chippy bundles gripped tight for clammy warmth on the dash home.

Demolition excavators with claws like dinosaur mouths pecked at parts of the Spindles Town Square Shopping Centre and chewed walls into rubble. As in Blackpool and indeed most towns erasing the 1960s, the site was hedged by wooden boards making promises. 'Watch this space,' they urged here, possibly with forefinger tapped on nose. 'You're looking at the creation of a bigger, better Spindles Town Square Shopping Centre.' Stalls from Tommyfield Market would be relocated there. It was the current Tommyfield I crooked my back and strolled towards now, on the trail of Mr Barlow's lofty claim.

At Market Place old acquaintances said fond hellos and gossiped on corners. Three old ladies exchanged health woes. 'Just wear and tear, doctor says,' said one. 'Oooh they always tell yer that, Elsie,' replied her friend. 'Then you put more pressure ont'other side walking funny, and it buggers that side an' all,' added the third. 'Still, could be worse,' they agreed, a phrase of great British making-do that always lifts my soul.

Close by, a Rastafarian man stood outside the travel agents' loudly singing reggae artist Burning Spear's lyrical destruction of colonialism, *Columbus*. It put Elsie's hip problems into perspective. To reach Tommyfield, I cut through an elegant arcade of empty shops. A man appeared as I paused. He urged me to look at a small wooden door up in the gable and asked, 'What do you think that's for, mate?' I said that I didn't know, and waited for an answer, intrigued. 'Me neither,' the man replied, before walking away. I hoped he was a tour guide.

The Tommyfield terrain is different now, its cobbles and flagstones from a more recent era. On the same soil beneath, though, and under similarly perplexing skies of stealth rain, the heart of Victorian Oldham throbbed here. Cotton mills had brought work for many and wealth for a few. The result was a fizzing, grimy boomtown. Around Tommyfield they gathered to chat and moan and play. Firewood sellers wearing top hats hawked their wares and men in flat caps supped from the town fountain. Even in such idle moments, work was omnipresent and physically inescapable. It was visible in the limps and hunchbacks of those who gathered and in the mill buildings that loomed close. These reminders tapped the shoulders of other workers too – on nearby Fairbottom Street could be seen the winding gear of Holebottom, a town centre colliery.

Many of those who gathered had finished work for the day. Factory bells signalled that much, and stomachs moaned and rumbled as a faint reinforcing echo. Then, in 1880, a new arrival trundled onto the scene. With a towering chimney and expansive wheels, John Rouse's steam-powered 'Dandy' resembled a model of an early railway locomotive. Rather than moving people or freight around, though, Rouse was providing a humanitarian service: Dandy was a mobile fish and chip range. No longer would the stomachs of Tommyfield wail.

There was, in that era, another peddler on the local scene – one who shunned recent industrial advancements. Newspaper reports identified him only as 'A stout man with a barrow drawn by a donkey' who led it 'through the streets, calling out his wares in a stentorian voice'. Both Dandy and donkey, though, were early adopters rather than pioneers, and so unlikely to be the ballast behind Mr Barlow's claim.

More plausible is that during those Selby twilight feasts he was referring to a Tommyfield tripe dresser named Mr Dyson. In one version of history, it was Dyson who, in the

1860s, first united fish with chips. Before this matchmaking, both fried fish and chipped potatoes had been consumed separately. Those who argued that Dyson was the cupid of batter and spud suggested that he had graduated from serving offal to fish almost by accident. In his 1972 book *Frying Tonight*, the journalist Gerald Priestland supposed that the pairing occurred because 'Chips were often sold by tripe-dressers,' and 'people sometimes brought cold pieces of fried fish to the chip shops to be warmed up by a quick plunge in the boiling fat'.

Down the years, others bolstered the red rose claim. In 1964, the White Fish Authority called for information about the origins of fish and chips and concluded that the two were first paired during 1865 in industrial Lancashire. Two years later, the circus performer Pierre Picton put his travels to virtuous use by compiling *A Gourmet's Guide to Fish & Chips*. This volume listed and detailed hundreds of chippies – an Egon Ronay guide for the masses – and included his agreement that fish wed chips in a Pennine mill town. Perhaps more controversially and certainly stereotypically, he proposed that the locals 'caught' their 'potato-eating habit from Irish immigrants'.

Whatever the veracity of their theories and Mr Barlow's proud boasts, the chippy trade undisputedly flourished in Oldham following those halcyon days of Dyson and donkeys. The great Edwardian fish and chip writer William Loftus (or 'Catchip', according to the byline beneath his columns) wrote that the town had 500 chip shops by the beginning of the twentieth century. Further, local factories and foundries had turned their men and machines to the manufacture of frying ranges. Alongside the dramatic spread of railways and technological advances in trawler fishing, their creations helped fuel the trade's expansion across Britain. Among those frying equipment firms was John Rouse (Oldham) Limited; the Dandy man had grown. Lancastrian companies like Rouse's also advanced frying technology so that offending stenches were diluted, diverted and nullified. It gave chip shop snobs one less thing to gripe over and helped begin the trade's journey from food of the poor to exalted national dish.

A plaque enlivens one penny-brown wall of the current Tommyfield Market building. It is a startling blue eye on an otherwise plain face. 'FISH AND CHIPS' cry the words that reel you in. They are followed by an explanation: 'Tommyfield, home of the first British fried chip. The first chips were fried in Oldham around 1860 from which the origins of Fish and Chip shops and the "Fast Food" industries can be traced.' Its authors did not stretch their claim as far as Mr Barlow, even if they wanted to. There is admirable modesty in that, but it also pertains to the fact that for a long time here and elsewhere (remember Dundee) they ate their chips without fish. There are even stories of battered fish being paired with jacket potatoes until the perfect combination was found. Perhaps various foods were trialled in the manner of someone streaking sample paints on a living room wall.

Oldham's chip plaque hangs next to Levers Fish & Chips, a Tommyfield institution. Today three French teenagers in rucksacks and baggy jeans read it and seemed to consider whether to eat from Levers' Takeaway or the adjacent Dining Room. That, or they were possibly exchange students saying 'My God, we took Chloe, Sarah and Jack to Paris and they've sent us somewhere that sells kidneys in a pie.'

I opted for the Dining Room. It was a perfect caff with one window to the outside world and another directly onto the indoor market stalls, like a giant fish tank. There were glowing greetings of 'Hiya, love' from two waitresses as I made my way from the door to a table. Next to me, two men in their seventies were finishing mugs of tea and a surprising snapshot drifted over the Formica divider between us. 'I've never met a Polish person I've not liked,' said one. 'How about General Jaruzelski?' replied his friend. There was some consideration before he calmly asserted, 'Well, I've not met him, have I, Paul?'

Glancing up from the menu, I realised that entertainment had unexpectedly unravelled in front of me, as on those glorious afternoons when a teacher would wheel out the school television and play a video for the rest of the lesson. I was audience now to a stage set fashioned by the windowed wall between Dining Room and Takeaway and performed upon by the animated fryers and waiting staff of Levers. Through a hatch, waitresses in their fire-extinguisher-red

T-shirts checked on orders with the men at the range. Their robes comprised the type of long white coat only worn by men of a certain age in the catering or butchering trades, and television drama doctors with a dubious past. Every few minutes one of them would exit stage left and reappear with their prop: a fresh fish, ready for its costume change. An ensemble cast of customers frequently breezed on to the set and could be seen contemplating their options with steadfast dedication. They awaited their food like relatives outside the labour ward, pacing and occasionally looking up from their phones to the frying range.

The windows and hatch were a drop scene speckled with backstories about people, place and time. Three lit menu boards included steak and kidney pudding and cheese and onion pie, placing us in Lancashire. One was dedicated entirely to options for children, hinting at how, outside of school bells, this was a place for family moments and nana treats. A printed sign promoted the £7.80 OAP special and cheerful handmade posters pushed Luxury Hot Chocolate and Luxury Ice Cream Milkshake, again perhaps singing of a place for all ages. Then came the framed pictures resting on a ledge. One showed half a dozen staff in white coats, proudly bearing battered cods speared by wooden forks, and another a black and white overhead photograph of Oldham. There too was an illustration of the grinning, white-bearded owner and a large photograph of a bespectacled man with the look of a friendly holiday waiter who pretends for the benefit of children that he can pull his thumb in two.

A smaller version of the image reappeared in another frame near a door that led to the market hall. It was part of a newspaper clipping slid into the glass frame next to a food allergies and intolerances notice. 'Tributes flood in for popular chippy worker' read its headline, and I felt a fleeting sadness for someone I'd never known.

Michael Solomon, the article revealed, had worked in Levers for fifteen years until shortly before his passing, aged 78. He was known for his cheery manner and for making 'customers feel welcome as they waited for their orders', to me an epitaph of worth and substance in a world where giant worries make brief moments of joy count double. Born in Cyprus, Michael's family had moved to Lancashire when he was a child. His Greek Cypriot relatives, in fact, have been custodians of Levers for some time. Theirs is an immigration pattern replicated across England; for many decades, Cypriots have been paramount to the fish and chip trade, vital actors in the manner of Scotland's Italians. Michael was one of them, and one of those many chip shop souls who float tiny bubbles of daft glee with their much-heard one-liners and crow's feet winks. They matter.

When I'd sat down, a waitress had asked 'Do you need a menu, love, or do you know what you want?' It was a line used each time a diner arrived and hinted at how this place breathed because of its regulars. Hardly a single person or couple who came in needed a menu. Most were greeted with a 'Pensioner's cod as usual is it, Peggy?' or 'Pudding and chips, Ernie flower?' Levers felt like a place of habit and retreat. Customers came in because they liked the food, of course, but this snug room was a haven. Popping by was a comforting ritual, not least for the lonely. Seemingly banal questions heard time and again – 'Any bread and butter, love?' – were soothers.

Down hovered my meal with an 'Enjoy' and a 'Definitely no bread and butter, love?' One cod end drooped over the plate's edge, reminding me of a child peeking under the bed to check for monsters. The fish was draped in a coat of waferish batter, a sort of gossamer bark to be whittled with cutlery rather than punctured and sawn. It made a crisp raft for the velvety cod. Where a bag of supermarket fries brings solid consistency, Levers' wonderful chips bloomed with individuality, each one a different size and shape to the next. Crispy tiddlers the shape of ironing boards hid beneath toppled fence posts and half-time satsuma segments. They tasted of home.

As I finished up, my plate now bald, a couple in their eighties shuffled in. After they had rested for a moment, the woman mentioned something about a birthday card and exited via the market door. A waitress asked the left behind husband if she'd be having the same as usual, and whether he wanted bread and butter with his pie and gravy. By the till, her colleague counted down someone's change but dropped a five-pound note while doing so. 'Awful, them new plastic ones are, especially wi' my nails,' she said. Again, I was left with the feeling of wanting a fish and chip shop to stay the same forever, just as we hope our grandparents will never pass away. Dyson, Dandy, Levers: you deserve more than a plaque.

The 343 from Oldham to Mossley was running late. A boarding passenger asked the driver, 'Do you go up past the Shepherd's Boy?' which presumably was the name of a pub rather than a permanently stationed farmer's son. 'I do, love,' he replied, 'now chop chop.' We bolted around a corner and almost missed a lady with partially purple hair waiting at the next stop. 'You didn't want to stop there,' she teased. 'You wanted to race because you're late.' 'Don't get cheeky cos you've been in't pub, love,' the driver countered. 'I don't drink!' came the retort. 'Gambling's my thing.' 'Oh well,' he concluded reflectively, 'We all need a thing.'

The bus groaned into the Pennine foothills. When particularly steep inclines were encountered, it made the noise of an irate vacuum cleaner. As we hurtled around tight country corners, I began to feel like a mail bag in the back of Postman Pat's van on a morning when he'd had a furious row with Mrs Goggins or done a line of coke.

Blackened old workers' cottages lined the roadside as we chugged closer still to the sky. The bus halted in Mossley and panted breathily, exhaling three of us out into the street opposite the Fleece Inn.

In 1863, local man John Lees returned to Mossley after a trip to Oldham. There, he had made a sensational discovery at Tommyfield Market: chips. The 28-year-old millworker was inspired. Alongside his wife, Lees ran the Enterprise Supper Bar from a wooden hut opposite The Fleece, or The Stamford Arms as it was then known. Now, the Enterprise's offering of pea soup with pigs' trotters would be supplemented with 'Chipped Potatoes in the French and American Style', as their sign read.

Towards the end of the nineteenth century, the Lees family moved their business across the road and into the premises of a former sweetshop at 41 Stamford Street. A 1902 black and white photograph shows John Lees outside the shop with two children, he and the eldest resplendent in white aprons. 'Lees's Chip Potato Restaurant', trumpet words handsomely painted onto its window, 'Oldest Estd. In the World.' Despite the words 'Fish and ...' being absent from the Lees sign, many have claimed 41 Stamford Street to be the very earliest chippy. Further, it has been contended that Lees was the first person to combine fish with chips, at the Enterprise in the 1860s.

Proof, as in the case of Dyson, is hard to find. The Lees argument hinges more on local pride and stories told by one generation to the next. In 1967, Mossley British Legion presented the shop with a Certificate of Authenticity that validated its claim; a year later, local historian Bob Worsnip backed those sentiments and relayed how a former owner's grandad had spoken of fish and chips being sold by Lees shortly after his Oldham epiphany. Those arriving in Mossley by rail now are greeted by a bright station mural depicting the Lees shop and its 'Oldest Estd.' avowal. Much

of the fish and chip story is built on instinct and feeling, and
the things your friend's dad says as you sit on a wall in Selby.
Folklore muddles the narrative but enriches it along the
way.

Half-a-dozen doors down from The Fleece, a sign
protrudes from the wall so that the first words any drinker
turning left spots are 'Fish + Chips'. They hang above
Man's Wok, for years now the locally beloved occupant of
41 Stamford Street. The combination of fish and chips and
Oriental food is not a new one. This is particularly so in
Lancashire and on Merseyside, where Chinese immigrants
have been reinvigorating the chippy trade for well over half
a century. Theirs is not an entirely gladdening story; many
Chinese people faced racism from the other side of the
frying range from the start. They were not always
welcomed by the traditional fish and chip industry either.
Gerald Priestland noted hostility among fryers here, though
his own use of the phrase 'The Yellow Peril' sits queasily
now.

On this Friday evening, Man's Wok radiated 'Chippy
Night' cheer. Customers' nostrils were seduced and mums
climbed from cars holding the chit list family order that they
already knew off by heart. The door and window that the
Lees had posed before was steamed up and for a minute I
could hear Mr Barlow's voice again. A boy who could not
have been much older than Richard and me on those
post-swimming streetlamp feasts said wearily of his sister:
'She'll get a meat pie but not eat the meat, as usual.'

Inside, customers pondered the menu wall, chefs rattled woks and steak and kidney puddings loafed in the steamers. 'Who's next please?' came a voice from behind the range. I ate my tea outside, of course.

5.

UP TO OUR HIPS IN ORANGE CHIPS

Wolverhampton and the Rhondda Valley

A woman in sunglasses that took up half of her face boarded the train at Stafford and began to photograph me. Her mobile phone camera swished a dozen times as she attempted various angles. I felt papped, but also irritated at the clangs of camera tones in a designated Quiet Coach. Mind you, I'd only realised it was the Quiet Coach as the couple sitting on the table across the aisle were whispering incredibly loudly so as not to be heard. 'Oh sorry,' said Sunglasses in my direction, 'I'm just taking a couple of selfies.'

Until the interruption, I'd been thinking about a fish and chip dispute in neighbouring Leicestershire. In 1986, a man named Peter Wood applied to open a chippy opposite a church in the village of Husbands Bosworth. Local authorities objected and refused permission. Wood responded quite naturally – he raised a sign on the intended site which read: 'The House of Erotica.' He felt it would sway minds; surely parishioners would prefer the sale of cod to dubious magazines? There is still no fish and chip shop in Husbands Bosworth.

Near Wolverhampton Station, an Evangelist preacher cheered us all up with his thoughts. 'When they bring in this digital money,' he ranted, 'they're gonna take away your credit cards and your debit cards. They're gonna put a chip in your hand and scan that, and the chip will be the Mark of the Beast.' 'Sounds bostin,'' replied a teenager as he passed by. 'Can I get two?'

On the West Midlands Metro – one of those systems served by modern, stylish trams that is so sleek you think it must be visiting from abroad – a single comma floated endlessly along the thin electronic destination name board. It felt like some kind of nihilistic statement. After the train's hermetic cocoon, hearing the dancing Wolverhampton accent was resuscitating. 'If ya get old, people just treat you old,' said a woman behind me. 'D'you know warra mean?' Her partner said nothing for a few seconds, and then, 'No. Not really.' Outside the window, workers in Blue Riband-wrapper overalls sucked on ciggies by a steel fabrication factory.

At Bilston, a Wolverhampton suburb with a life all of its own, there were further steely markers. Rising from the tram station, the visitor is greeted first by a gable end sign for Chaplin's Fish & Chips, and then by beautiful engravings of social and industrial memories. 'The sky lit up in a big burst of red glow,' declares one, recalling Bilston Steelworks. The soot may have lifted, but Black Country pride still resounds.

Residents basked in the sun and asked of passerby acquaintances, 'How's your Marion?' or 'Have you seen Pete lately?' I marvelled at the vintage solidity of Morton's Army and Navy Store and AR White & Son, purveyors of gents clothing since 1929, and felt the calm a small town bestows.

Bilston Market enhanced this feeling of blessed normality. Dave's Frozen Deals urged visitors to 'Forget the thrills, save on your bills!' and at Matt the Baker's a woman meticulously specified the exact pork pie she required from the fridge. Shoppers worked through their lists or thought long and hard about the impromptu purchase of Elvis clocks or soft velour football team facecloths. Two colleagues at a butchers' stand erupted into laughter. 'Oh no, she's got a feather up her arse again,' called across a woman selling greeting cards. Then a baby in a buggy pointed to me and screamed, several times over, 'Dada! Dada! Dada!' so I moved on.

Outside, a man on an e-scooter careered along the pavement. People scattered as if parting for Clark Kent sprinting towards a phone box. A pensioner sitting on a bench by the library shook his head and spoke all of our thoughts. 'What a prick,' he said. I began to yearn for the relative safety of Blackpool mobility scooters. But all annoyance melted when I spotted my destination: Major's.

Major Spencer and his partner Olive opened their fish and chip shop here in 1975. Now run by son Royston, Major's is one renowned producer of a Black Country-wide delicacy: the Orange Chip. Since the middle of the twentieth century, shops here have been dousing their uncooked chips in a batter that includes paprika, orange colouring or turmeric depending on who you ask, and then frying them. The result, say those bred here, is an upgrade, a crispy chip far superior to its blander, regular cousin; a sublime, fluorescent renegade whose sampling can lead only to addiction. The Orange Chip has become a totem of Black Country identity and another thing to differentiate this proudly separate region from Birmingham.

In keeping with the narrative of the wider fish and chip story, nobody knows who invented the orange chip, or where, or when, or why. Perhaps they were designed to reflect those glowing steelworks, or celebrate the colours of Wolverhampton Wanderers, although any Walsall or West Bromwich Albion supporter would retch at such a thought. All is vague, save for a few impassioned claims like that of the Black Country Chippy in Great Bridge, between West Bromwich and Dudley. Fryers there asserted that their grand-father was the main alchemist, some time in the late 1940s. Then running a previous family chippy in the town, he had concocted orange chips almost by accident while using up leftover batter late at night. Post-pub customers tried them and from then on demanded their chips in the neon fashion.

No matter their derivation, a mural inside Major's saluted this 'Home of fine fish and the battered chip', enticement enough for me. Trying one – and this, perhaps, is a measure of my own personal and moral bankruptcy – excited me. Here was something new, a variation, cultural enrichment. Plus, it was basically a chip dressed in scraps.

Beneath its black and orange logo, I entered bustling Major's where a disorderly queue fumbled its way along the counter to the back of the shop. Thankfully, an old lady arrived to vanquish this nightmare scenario, organising patrons into a neat and tidy line. She didn't work there, and I am not even sure that she joined herself or was even dining, but we remained thankful. Perhaps she marshals chippy queues across the Midlands before disappearing, a Mary Poppins with an umbrella shaped like a giant wooden fork.

While waiting, I read a printed banner strewn across a wall beam. 'Ah you think batter is your ally?' it asked. 'You merely adopted the batter. I was born in it, moulded by it ...', continuing for a line or two and then concluding, 'The batters betray you, because they belong to me.' Somewhat impressed by the banner's poetic prowess, I searched the words on my phone. It turned out to be an adaptation of some dialogue from a Batman film, *Dark Night Rises*, in which various words for darkness and light had been substituted with 'batter'.

As a Carpetright sale advert blazing from Heart FM argued with the melodious frying ranges, I looked along the queue and over to the Major's dining area. Once again, the universality of the chip shop congregation struck. There was a nana and her granddaughter, a poor distraught mite whose wailing could not even be halted by an orange chip. A young woman wearing a hijab grabbed blindly at a box of chips while fixated on her phone. Standing in front of me, a council worker held his tenner in the air as if he were on some stock exchange floor, and a middle-aged woman battled a bunch of helium 'Happy 60th' balloons to prevent them absconding out of the door. 'Have a Bostin' Day' offered handwritten words on a chalkboard atop the frying range, and somehow, for those fifteen minutes at least, I felt that we all were.

'What can I get you, bab?' asked one of the two Major's women between counter and frying range. Both were dynamos, apparently taking orders, frying, scooping food and poking the card payment machine or issuing change all at the same time, their arms a cartoon whirlwind. It occurred to me now that orange chips were not a gimmick or a novelty, nor a deep-fried Mars bar Stonehaven tourist attraction; they were *the* chips, the only ones on offer, with no special line on the menu or indeed even a mention of the word orange. Like an overawed child meeting a celebrity, I waffled aimlessly about this being my first orange chip encounter. 'Well, you'll enjoy them, love. Best ones, those.'

Waiting in the queue, I'd enjoyed the differing verses of people's orders and then the consistent choruses from those serving them. As in all chippies, the staff spoke in questions – 'Open or wrapped?', 'Any sauces with that?', 'Is that the regular or large haddock?' These, of course, varied according to order and location, but one remained consistent across most areas: 'Salt and vinegar?' It was a constant, a familiar and welcome gesture like a wave from a child watching your train. This romantic view does not work both ways. Having to ask this question so many times per shift can perhaps only be withstood by switching into pilot mode. In a chip shop on the outskirts of my hometown, York, I'd recently chatted with a counter lady who had found herself repeating 'Do you want salt and vinegar?' in her sleep. 'It was one of the reasons me and my boyfriend split up,' she'd added. I'd probably have proposed.

The West Midlands were an apt place to think about condiments. Whole reservoirs of vinegar are distributed from hereabouts. Look carefully – though without squeezing acidic matter into your eye as I once did – at one of those bulbous dispensers that reside on chip shop counters and tables across the land and you'll see the words: 'Drywhite Ltd of Halesowen Traditional Fish & Chip Shop Taste Vinegar.' Since 1933, Drywhite have been helping to enliven our suppers.

The manner in which chip shop customers dress their meals fascinates me. Somehow, probably through decisions made in childhood and fully influenced by parents or in opposition to siblings, we have decided that, yes, we like 'loads' of salt and vinegar, or we like 'a little' vinegar but a lot of salt, or 'just salt', or – and, frankly these people scare me – neither. A downside of Mr Barlow's beloved outside eating is the worry that a server will fail in their task, either under-garnishing a meal due to differing definitions of 'loads', or drowning and suffocating its contents. All of us should, perhaps, be a bit like my Aunty Angela, who for a while ran a chip shop in Middlesbrough. She carries condiments sachets in her handbag under the fine reasoning, 'Well, you just never know, do you?'

Others add further trimmings – tartare sauce, ketchup, salad cream (monsters). Everyone knows *their* way of consuming food from a chippy. It is customised, claimed and adorned like no other cuisine. There are regional variations – curry sauce or gravy, heathen additions in some places, necessary embellishments in others; or the previously mentioned chippy sauce which is essential in Edinburgh but jilted in Glasgow.

Orange chip land is, naturally, the place to consider other regional variations, those chip shop nuances that rarely travel outside certain regions or communities. There is London with its pickled wallies – large bowed gherkins with strong immigrant origins like the city they serve and a name derived from rhyming slang. Hull has American Chip Spice, a paprika powder scattered at the counter and perhaps mirroring the port city's tradition of looking out to the world. We have already experienced puddings red and steak in Scotland and Lancashire respectively, barms and butties, plus scallops and fritters and Yorkshire fishcakes to name but three fried variants. Others exist – Cumbrian chippies with their mash and mince patties, Hull again with its own 'slapped' potato patties – and sometimes it is only when we travel to chippies in other locales that we realise not everywhere is the same. A friend of mine moved to Manchester, ordered his usual battered sausage and chips only to be told, 'We don't do that here.'

Some trends cover wider terrain. Mushy peas were considered northern though now seem ubiquitous. Northerners fried in dripping and southerners oil. Further, there have long been regional traditions in the type of fish certain places sell. In 1957, *The Times* newspaper proposed that 'Lancashire and South Wales, for example, prefer hake, in Leeds and the West Riding haddock is a prime favourite, Scotland likes small haddock, and in London and the south skate and rock salmon tend to be more popular.' Today, Scotland and the West Riding remain loyal to haddock, it would appear, but there is a more mixed scene elsewhere in the north and more variety the further south travelled. Even then, there is not harmony on whether to leave fish skin on or off. My maternal grandad, an often cantankerous but admirably particular Yorkshireman, adored fish and chips. However, each time he entered a chippy he would ask, 'Do you leave the skin on?' If an affirmative answer followed, then that shop's proprietors were likely to be denounced as 'Dirty bastards.'

Not that he would have used the word 'Chippy'; rather – and always – 'Fish shop', the same phrase my dad uses. In other places 'Chipper' is the word. This is not the only aspect of fish and chips language which varies. My beloved scraps are elsewhere known as 'Bits', 'Gribbles', 'Scrantions', 'Screeds', 'Scrumps' and 'Scratchings'. Scottish friends and family eat not a bag of chips, but a 'poke'. Some north-easterners have been known to call a fish supper a 'fish lot' and Welsh people dub a portion of chips a 'bechdan'. It is clear, then, that the national dish embodies the complexities and eccentricities of its population and their multi-faceted identities. And that we just really, really like frying stuff.

I was gladder than ever of these regional differences as I sat on a bench outside Major's. If orange chips had travelled beyond their Black Country borders, the food now resting in a box on my knee would not have been novel. Indeed, I would not have been drawn to Bilston, where a busker's soulful singing now sailed through the air like a pleasant alarm, and where I could enjoy the comings and goings at the Horse and Jockey pub opposite. It looked like a vintage daytime pub where it was still possible to buy forty-eight eggs or some Levi's jeans from a man named Smudger or Dodgy Ken.

In-between the bench and the boozer was a statue sculpted to commemorate the toils of women steel and metal workers. I opened the box and it was as if tiny molten sparks were seeping out in unity. The batter debris clung to the chips, dayglo limpets. That something so familiar appeared suddenly so different recalled the first encounter with a loved one after they've had a radical haircut. It was as if the sun was setting on the chips and here was some berserk, radiating treasure chest rather than a cardboard vessel. Admittedly, there was also a hint of the nuclear, something enhanced by the faint whiff of old radio speakers that occasionally wafted upwards.

Any misgivings faded with the first bite. Agreeable, sweet crunch surrendered to fuzzy, scorching fluff. Orange chips did not necessarily taste *better* than normal chips; they just tasted *more*. Their sparky tang accompanied the usual flavours of comfort, an update on perfection. A turbaned man with a walking stick clinked slowly by and smiled. 'Oh they look good,' he said. 'I might have to join you.'

'We've taken such a number of beatings in our time,' said the Welshman. 'National identity lost. The language lost, a large part of the religion lost. But I think we'll put on a Custer's Last Stand for the potato and the chip.' It was 1962 and Gwyn Thomas, playwright and author, stood in a Rhondda Valley chip shop doorway being interviewed for BBC television's *Tonight* programme. His interrogator, Alan Whicker, had been dispatched to report on a national chip crisis. 'Think of Italy without pasta,' he'd begun his piece, 'China without rice, France without wine. Here the fish and chip shops are the pillar upon which society rests.'

Whicker explained that a bitter winter had killed off or delayed much of the potato crop. Now the threat of fish without chips was imminent. Elsewhere, Mr H.S. Dawes of the Burton and District Fish Fryers' Association warned how that town's forty shops would soon close, some permanently. Slightly more exotically, an Italian newspaper also covered the emergency, claiming that 'The beloved dish' had 'vanished from many a table.' For this 'traditional meal of the working classes' to be sold without chips would be, in their eyes, a travesty akin to macaroni without cheese. The

Italians even carried reports of British people suggesting that spaghetti should be used as a substitute.

This would afflict all of Britain's chippies – up to 14,000 of them – of course. However, according to Whicker, the Welsh ate fish and chips on a greater scale than anyone else, and so the crisis would cause the most profound impact upon them. In this area, he relayed, there was one chip shop for every 2,000 people. Importing potatoes as had been suggested would quadruple prices, 'a national calamity'.

Even in a black and white film clip the glint in Gwyn Thomas's eye is obvious. There is certainly some poetic exaggeration at play, and a sense that he is toying with Whicker. Yet every time I watch I am transfixed by his performance and convinced there is some meaning – and certainly feeling – behind the quixotic bluster.

Thomas remembers, or claims to, the 'chip shop keepers' of his youth as 'a very compassionate race of people' who rewarded poetry recital and song from queuing customers. 'I received free chips for at least four years of my life,' he avows. Then the whimsy gives way to rather dark analysis: 'The chip is the most polite and pleasant way of starving, and we've been invited to starve on many occasions in our historical career.' Thomas elaborates how the mass consumption of chips 'With salt which kills, with vinegar which apparently kills ... was the quickest way out.'

He diverts next to religion, suggesting that the Welsh obsession with chips is a rebellion against 'All of the revivals which warned us against sex and sin ... We wanted this great unstiffening, and we found it in starch, and we have been up to our hips in chips ever since. A great need, this is what music is to the Italians and statues to the Greeks.'

Thomas then considers a chip-less future, explaining how confusion will reign among the Welsh for a while, but then they will go 'back to the fields, back to the hillsides, where we will be able to produce potatoes the size of footballs. And without any need for lacing them up either.' The film cuts here, possibly because he is smirking, but through words and pictures, whether wry or genuine, a clear image of a place that cares about its chips has emerged. The Rhondda Valley looks like my kind of region.

To reach the land of Gwyn Thomas, I left the Black Country and travelled south-west. A mildly perturbing incident occurred in the Gents toilets at Bristol Temple Meads just as I was minding my own business, remembering how that city had been home to Britain's first electronic fish and chip vending machine in 1984. From behind me a voice asked, 'Have you been a good girl for Daddy?' and 'Are you going to dance later?' Alarmed, I turned to find a businessman on his phone and went back to thinking about vending machines.

At Cardiff Queen Street, Tannoy recordings and live announcements in English and Welsh congealed into a mess so that it sounded as if 'the next Trafnidiaeth Cymru service for Bae Caerdydd would be departing in do not leave your luggage unattended we are sorry to announce ...' A number of tables on the train to Pontypridd appeared to be suffering from mange; a network of barren patches had been scraped from the veneer by passengers. The moquette seats discharged notes of musty jumble-sale clothing, and there was a general feeling that touching surfaces was inadvisable. 'I'm going to sleep so I'm not really here,' said a teenage girl to her boyfriend.

The carriage's interior swiftly stopped mattering as the train huffed into the countryside. Outside, this corridor of south-east Wales blazed with beauty. Great verdant mountains emerged suddenly, forming happy stripes with the blue sky. Homes were built on and among them. At Taffs Well, so otherworldly was the perspective that one mountain seemed to be playing hide and seek in between two houses, a friendly and misunderstood monster on the run.

My search for Gwyn Thomas's cradle of chips would mean boarding a Rail Replacement Bus – few words in the English language are more feared – at Pontypridd for Porth. Our wagon gasped into the Rhondda Valley, with its blend of bygone industry in the form of decomposing winding gears, low broad workers' terraced houses and rural beauty. The River Rhondda flowed beside us, a constant in all phases of this region's life, though no doubt cleaner now than when chimneys belched and miners hacked.

In Porth a man exited the Empire Café with a twenty-pound note clenched tight in his teeth, flapping in the breeze. For a few seconds I thought he had a rabid tongue. This was a languid town of the type those with families feel happily settled in and those under the age of 25 yearn to flee. There was a Woolworths repurposed as a greetings card shop, a nightclub called Squares, a vacuum cleaner repair shop whose window taught me it was possible to be nostalgic about Hoovers and a disused cinema latterly used as a bingo hall. It languished on a corner opposite two fish and chip shops, and the ghostly shell of a good night out could be imagined. Although Porth was pleasant enough, as in the train carriage, its appearance did not matter due to its surroundings; in every direction, steady and curvaceous mountains supplied both drama and calm.

I crossed over the Rhondda to Cymmer, which to an outsider like me was seemingly joined with Porth, but no doubt fiercely defended as a village in its own right by residents. Perhaps it was telling that, in Porth, as I carried some shopping to a bus stop for an old lady (she was catching a bus from there and did ask me to do so, I should point out), I asked her how to correctly pronounce Cymmer, spelling the word out. She thought for a while and then replied: 'Never heard of it.'

Gwyn Thomas was born at 196 High Street, Cymmer, in 1913. At the bottom of that hilly road I began my search for his home, stopping every once in a while to check my progress by looking at the numbers on houses. At one point, a lady waved heartily at me from her living room and I felt guilty for not being her long lost son. I paused to look down a side street at the neat Cymmer Colliery Workingmens

Institute, whose bar and function rooms Thomas must have known. 'Morning. Or is it afternoon? Doesn't matter when it's sunny, does it?' said a lady walking her dog.

Chapel and pub were at the centre of life in the Rhondda Valley. Cymmer's, on opposing corners, had both closed down. Davies' and Thomas' graves had no congregation to pray for them, and the fag ash box of the boarded-up hostelry had been left hanging open like a robbed safe. A tirade of cars swarmed on the next part of the High Street, stealing my concentration until I spotted a modest grey plaque beneath a sizeable satellite dish: Gwyn Thomas, Author, 1913–1981, Was Born Here.

At the Thomas family gate, I turned and saw that the blackened terraced houses opposite looked remarkably like those from which Alan Whicker had introduced the 1962 film. I followed the course of his piece-to-camera amble, the shade on that side adding a sepia tint. Quickly, my eyes met The Cymmer Fish Bar. A chippy, and within sniffing distance of Thomas's doorstep. Perhaps his words were not exaggerated.

Even without my head bowed and senses drowned by vehicle din, The Cymmer Fish Bar would have been difficult to spot. In a fine old but disappearing tradition, it was essentially the front room of a terraced house. Of four windows upstairs and down, only one belonged to the chippy. A domestic door ushered customers through a porch, over the threshold and in. Laughter fluttered outwards from within now; perhaps a customer was performing poetry for free chips. Regulars stepped into the street, looking back with a

'See you next week' and then forwards to those of us waiting outside with an 'Alrigh', how's it goin'?'

The Cymmer Fish Bar's modest room had enough personality to stock a warehouse. From behind a compact frying range burbling rhythmically, two cheery women ran the show. If one of them already knew a customer's regular order then the other had supplementary information to offer – 'He likes it in a tray, and he likes plenty of salt and vinegar. And charge him by the grain.' They were also consummate professionals, barely even flinching when the man in front of me asked for his fish to be doused in gravy, which is surely some kind of criminal act.

Everything existing in close proximity meant that a customer was immersed in the shop rather than being a passive bystander waiting to be served. It felt like we were almost inside the condensation-smudged range window, and among the pale gold batter. It also meant that I was close enough to spy scraps behind the fog: my most southernly sighting ever. The magnitude of this revelation stunned me, resulting in an incoherent opening sentence of 'Hello. Can I have scraps, please?' Just as I thought the kindly lady was about to ask if I'd come out without my carer, she replied, 'Scrumps? Yes, sweetheart. Do you want anything with them?' Composing myself enough to add fish and chips to my scrumps, I marvelled at the speed of her wrapping. It was mesmeric, a martial art or a magician's sleight of hand. I felt like applauding but was pretty sure the authorities had already been alerted about my behaviour.

Sitting on a wall opposite the shop, I untangled her work. I'd managed to gather myself enough to order a can of Vimto, that sensible, mature adult version of a Bubblegum Panda Pop. The drink had been on my mind since I'd passed through Manchester en route to Oldham. There I'd encountered A Monument To Vimto. This statue of a giant Edwardian Vimto bottle with its orange label ('Invigorating. The Ideal Beverage.') is situated where the drink was once produced. It is surrounded by giant renderings of grapes and raspberries, two key Vimto ingredients. The drink was conceived as an alternative to alcohol during a post-Victorian Temperance craze. Dandelion and Burdock, a similarly sublime fish and chips accompaniment and always my first choice, has similar origins. In any case, to true traditionalists like my mum either option is heretic, a cup of tea being the righteous choice.

From a makeshift chip paper tablecloth spread across my lap, I began eating. 'This is the great culmination of human experience: the chip,' Thomas had said in the Whicker video. 'This warm savoury thing which will never betray you as adultery might, which will never inspire you unduly as art might, the chip is life itself.' At that moment on a stumpy wall in Cymmer, such hyperbole resonated. These chips, clouded in bubbly cumulus scrumps, were wondrous. In the beating valley sun, globules of vinegar shimmered on their straw-yellow backs. They tasted of some forgotten yesterday, and isn't that just the very point of this meal, that it can throw you through time and place? The fish worked in symphony, its fine batter in the hue of a sun lotion bottle giving way to incandescent cod.

With my allocation of chips beyond generous to the point of being a philanthropic act, I was unable to consume the lot. It is always hard to stop – just one more, and maybe those three little crispy ones – a habit that recalls lovelorn telephone calls of 'No, you hang up first' goodbyes. Scrunching up my papers in the clumsy manner of someone unable to fold up an OS map, I headed back to Cardiff. A coating of grease clung to the roof of my mouth. I considered it a temporary memorial to Gwyn Thomas, silver-tongued bard of Welsh chippies.

6.

TOMORROW'S CHIP PAPER

Cardiff and Brixham

It is nearly midnight on Chippy Lane, Cardiff. Drinkers stumble towards The Food Studio or Fellas and ponder window portraits of posing kebabs and pouting burgers, hot dogs and fish and chips. No one quite knows which meal this is – A second tea? A late supper? An early breakfast? – but they need it. Delivery couriers on bikes slalom among them and a man balances his spent takeaway carton on top of an overflowing bin with the precision of a keyhole surgeon playing Jenga. A woman emerges from the Corner House pub, smacks together her hands and announces her plans. 'Chips and then home,' she says. 'Perfect.'

Stickered words in a window of Dorothy's Fish Bar offer poetry: 'Heinz Baked Beans/Grated Cheddar Cheese/Batchelor's Mushy Peas ...' A loose and clumsy queue has mustered and they inch towards the blazing glow inside, passing beneath letters that declare 'Est 1953.' In truth, they are more likely to order Dorothy's famous delicacies of spit roasted chicken curry off the bone, or chips with cheese blanketed in curry sauce or gravy. The latter will then be adorned with a luminously-crumbed rissole of mash, onion and corned beef. This addition was bequeathed to Wales by Italian immigrants, although Dorothy's was founded by the Greek Cypriot Stavri family and remains theirs. Such diversions once more whisper to us that our beloved chippies bloomed on the graft of people from far away.

Tonight, other Chippy Lane diners float next door to Tony's Fish Bar, perhaps transfixed by its neon aquarium lighting. Tony's also claims septuagenarian status: 'EST 1953' barks a blood-red message on its sign. Sitting on a chair outside, a lad in his late teens surrenders a deluge of ketchup onto his pale blue shirt then mops it up with a chip like someone attempting to turn back the tide with a bucket and spade. A seagull looks on from the seat opposite, very possibly shaking its head in disapproval.

There are ten or so takeaways on this narrow, pedestrianised strip of not much more than 100 metres in length. Alternatively nicknamed 'Chip Alley' – depending on who you ask – the road's real name is Caroline Street. For many decades this has been a staging post on nights out in Cardiff or, more commonly, the last stop before a dawdling walk or a testy cab ride ('No Hot Food in Taxi …') home. Its unofficial renaming hints at a universal truth: there are few greater chips than the post-pub chip. Soaking up much of what has gone before and even sobering us up a little, the late-night chippy visit cleanses and restores, a fifteen-minute spa break for a couple of quid. From light to dark we go, eyes fixed and steam climbing.

That said, we need not be half merry or tanked up to enjoy late chips in the dark. There is a faint decadence about doing so, and a sense of cosiness. We walk along with our toasty bouquet, a comforting companion, and we are completely and blissfully distracted. It has long been this way, even in the most troubling of times. In November 1939, a Yorkshireman named Frank Turner was fined *10s* for eating fish and chips after 11pm during the blackout period. Turner forgot that he was holding a torch in his hand, and a police officer spotted it beaming into the sky each time he raised his hand to eat.

On Chippy Lane and every strip like it, teeming and tumultuous late nights and early mornings shriek of a takeaway economy in fine fettle. The crisis of 1962 feels sharply distant. Ditto while waiting in healthy queues at Mossley or Bilston. Yet this industry is rarely far from strife, something uncomfortably obvious during my travels. At the York fish and chip shop where the server offered salt and vinegar in her sleep, one customer had summed up the threat by asking his companion, 'Have you heard how many chippies are closing? It's terrifying.' 'I know,' the friend replied. 'Better make mine a large one.'

Then there had been Val D'Oro, and Gianluca's mention of dizzying ingredient and energy price rises, an understandably common conversational theme among fryers. In the months prior to my visiting Wolverhampton, Major's had suffered a tripling in fish and potato costs, and a quadrupling in oil charges. The National Federation of Fish Friers (NFFF), for more than a century considered the impressive and authoritative voice of the industry, then aired concerns that vastly inflated potato prices could force many chippies to close.

Solace will not pay their bills but a smidgen of comfort can be found in remembering that the fish and chip industry has long been doughty and resilient. This spirit was exemplified in 1939. That year a Withernsea chip shop owner evaded Sunday trading restrictions by inventing a fish and chip dispensing machine. He secretly manned the contraption himself; we can only hope that he made accompanying robotic noises.

In the past, the fish and chip industry survived those years of smite and derision from lofty types and fought back after having been defined as an Offensive Trade. Now, it continues to compete in a culinary landscape more varied and cosmopolitan than ever. To look back down the decades is to encounter multiple crises, whether competition from curry or Chinese food, further potato and chip shortages in 1975 and 1999, moral panics about European Union 'bureaucrats' who are about to 'bow to Spanish fishermen' with the effect of calamitous rises in the price of cod, or frequently repeated stories about young people avoiding chippies in pursuit of more exotic venues and cuisines. A glance through archive television and radio listings reveals programmes that ask, 'Why is fish and chips almost a dish of the past?' or explain 'Fish and chips – How the real stuff is under threat.'

Every few years, tabloid headlines such as 'Shark and Chips?' surface. The articles which follow suggest that depleted cod or haddock stocks could soon lead to alternatives being served up by chip shops. Beneath the bombast, there are tidings here that are beyond dispute: ocean sustainability matters. I decided the time had come to roam beyond the Severn and into Devon, in search of the future of fish and chips. After I'd had a deep-fried nightcap from Dorothy's, naturally.

A decade ago, when my daughter was four, we took a family holiday in Padstow. One late afternoon I was feeling flush, having found a £20 note on the ground. Unclaimed, it had fluttered spasmodically like a maimed butterfly and she performed a little dance around it. The two of us were deeply into our fish and chips excursions by then and so we tried Rick Stein's fish and chip restaurant, close to Padstow harbour. Until that moment, I had not known that such a place existed and that fish and chips could be eaten in such lavish, contemporary surroundings. Neither had I encountered so much consideration, so much *thought*, being dedicated to the dish's ingredients, provenance and presentation. When our meals arrived, they looked different

– cleaner, slighter than usual, and appetising but in a reserved and refined manner. The fish and chips I knew were heartier and more ample. Stein's were the acoustic version.

The next day we joined the queue at Chip Ahoy, a back-street shop crammed between crooked cottages. On one creviced wall was a rhythmic list of former owners, like a bowling club's roll call of champions: Ida Bat, Horace Jones, Peggy and Fred Norfolk, Stan and Cherry Withbread. It felt natural and soulful to me in a way Stein's hadn't. Later, pottering in a graveyard, we encountered an old sailor returning from there. For certain strangers, a child is an inducement to tell stories, a welcome windfall of parenting that nobody tells you about. He recounted to us the boats he had crewed and the storms he had seen. Then, the sailor held up his Stein's takeaway. 'Children's portion,' he said. 'I got there and it's all I could bloody afford.'

Stein's had been a happy, breezy experience and yet inverse snobbery and northern prickle left me feeling uneasy. Besides, even money falling from the sky could not disguise the expense of eating there in comparison to a regular chippy. There was an undeniable sense that places like this were the future, but I worried that in this guise fish and chips would become unobtainable for less well-off people who, after all, had been the dish's most loyal consumers from the very start. Was the Stein's rendering of a chippy what the Daily Telegraph had in mind with their 'classless' claim, made that same year? That is, 'classless' in the sense that all classes now had their own versions of fish and chips, along the lines of Victorian railway carriages?

Arriving in neighbouring Devon, Torquay prised free earlier memories of family holidays. For a number of years when I was a child, my parents would drive us here from York. In our spluttering Austin Princess, we'd set off around midnight and arrive far too early to check in at our bed and breakfast. As a morning mizzle spattered my face now, I recalled glancing through raindrops that had convened on the car window and across to the ashen sea. For now, last night's spam sandwiches, tepid and compressed, were all that was on offer to silence mine and my sisters' growling stomachs. Later, there would be chips, that simplest yet most alluring of promises.

Down by the marina, The Great British Fish and Chip Shop awaited customers to feed. Perhaps touristic appetites had been reduced by time spent in the attraction next door. The Real Crime Museum, with its promises of 'Letters from killers', 'Krays memorabilia' and 'Original murder weapons', hardly seemed a traditional seaside pastime. I did not find out if it was cheerier than it sounded because I had a boat to find.

Earlier, when buying a ticket for the Western Lady ferry to Brixham, the friendly teenager who took my money had asked, 'So it's literally just you?' Once more, the seaside was doing its best to scream the word 'LONER' at me. There was to be no redemption in the company of strangers once I had mistakenly jumped the boarding queue while trying to escape earshot of an infernal game of I-Spy that two young siblings were playing. For the entire half-hour crossing, I could feel eyes lasering into the back of my head – I had taken the best seat, at the front, obviously.

There was nothing dismal about the English Channel today, and earlier rainclouds had skedaddled elsewhere. Now blues heavy and light met on the horizon, school exercise books stacked on a shelf. The ocean rolled and tilted *The Western Lady*. Looking across I thought of those who venture out to sea so that our chippies have cod or haddock to batter.

Brixham fish market earns more for its sales than any other in England, almost £61m in 2022, mostly via internet auction. The town has lived from what it catches for hundreds of years. Its seamen helped pioneer developments in trawling that would eventually hasten the spread of fish and chip shops across the nation. From 1850, the town had this country's largest trawling fleet. Soon their catch was being moved across the land by rail, further helping to propel the Victorian chippy boom. Brixham fishermen faced the sea's dark perils unaided by engine power until the 1930s. Little wonder they looked to the skies for protection, always making Sunday chapel worship even if that meant mooring up far from home.

Being a Brixham seaman remains a tough profession stalked by danger. In the harbour now, a canvas banner hangs from a wall. It depicts a waving fisherman in his yellow overalls and a mother holding their child. 'Home Misses You Too,' reads the text. 'Get back home and dry for them.'

The Western Lady advanced on Brixham. The town's hillside houses grew larger with each blink of an eye. Some were painted in seaside rock shades that brightened and focused in tandem, as if 20p had been fed into clifftop viewing binoculars. Arriving somewhere by sea is a gradual and joyful drama for the casual traveller. Imagine the exquisite wave of gladness a returning fisherman must feel.

As it entered the harbour, the ferry's engine sang in throaty glugs after the low whine of progression at sea. Day boats bobbed and trawlers slowly swayed, serene for now. Above them, the Fish Market was silent too.

Some perched on the harbour wall and some on benches behind the open concertina windows of the takeaway. They jabbed forks at chips and snapped batter with their fingers, then they looked upwards and out to the boats. Eating this meal right here seemed correct and appropriate. It enriched the experience, the fish and chips version of devouring a margherita in Naples or a hotdog from a chrome New York stall on wheels. Except, this wasn't another country's cuisine; it was theirs. Much about this nation had made many people sad or angry in recent times. Right now, though, for a few precious moments there were not many better places to be or foods to be eating. Deep fried objects and the English Riviera provided temporary bliss.

Their food had come from Rockfish Brixham, one of several waterside outlets operated by the same company across Devon and Dorset. Rockfish greatly consider the sustainability of what they serve, all of which is provided by Brixham Fish Market. Such ethics cost. As Rockfish founder and CEO Mitch Tonks told BBC Radio's *The Food Programme* in 2013, even a decade ago rising prices were inevitable: 'Fish and chips obviously used to be cheap, it was post-war, everybody was eating fish and the trouble is, everybody thinks fish should be cheap.' Whether it was the mellowing of age, our growing ecological awareness or the fact that such economic realities were now besetting all types of fish and chip purveyors, I found myself more sympathetic to this view than in my harsh and hackled judgement of Stein's. Mind you, I still wouldn't have minded finding a £20 note to put towards my tea.

Looking upwards and muttering my apologies to Mr Barlow, I went inside to eat. Parquet flooring – which always makes me want to take off my shoes and skid as in the school assembly hall – led to wooden steps. White brick walls were clad with a merchandise cabinet and framed photographs of fish and family. All of it shone bountifully under the light from a wide observation window that offered an enlarged periscope view of the harbour. 'Daniel?' said the affable woman who checked my reservation. 'Welcome. Table for one, isn't it?' 'Yes, it's literally just me,' I replied.

Out on the harbour balcony, it was difficult to concentrate on the menu. Below in the water, a sequence of small boats were returning, birds back to their nests. Trawlermen fixed ropes while the sun further creosoted their faces. The distant tinkling of buoys occasionally trickled over, a faulty jewellery box being opened and closed.

A waiter arrived, said his kind hellos, and then listed 'Today's Seafood Market catch' specials to those of us in the vicinity. His delivery was impeccable, the recital perfect. However, I drifted in and out, as when someone tells a long joke. I wrongly thought 'It comes with bream salad' was my prompt to speak, but it turned out that the waiter had not yet told us what an 'Amazing, silky fish' the Ray Wing is. I ordered from the Traditional Fish & Chips section of the main menu, which was probably even more of a faux pas than compensation-laughing too enthusiastically at the correct end of the long joke.

As the haddock wore a skin and I did not want my grandad's ghost to appear at my shoulder denouncing me, I ordered White Ling. It was, according to the menu, 'A delicious white fish similar to cod,' served in accordance with the company's ethical principles. Certainly, Ling constituted an exotic choice for me, one I'd not knowingly eaten before. I had very possibly consumed it *unknowingly* from one of those chippies whose vague menu boards simply offer 'Fish'. I thought of a friend who used to comment, 'What does it matter anyway, once it's covered in batter?' and felt glad he wasn't present to say it now. Doing so would have been a bit like lighting a ciggy on a petrol forecourt.

Rockfish did not feel like a Shaw's Dandelion and Burdock or a Vimto kind of place. Blaming the blue ocean for cultivating in me that precious holiday feeling, I ordered a glass of white wine, perhaps risking another ghostly visitation ('Fish and chips, with *wine*?!'). It arrived in a Rockfish-branded glass, sibling to Rockfish-branded condiments dispensers, all of them splashed in teal, the main Rockfish shade. The smart uniformity was pleasing, but not an elevation on what had been plonked down in front of me elsewhere. Just different. In fact, after one sip I began to think of the white disposable cup that Enrico had placed upside down on top of my Fanta can, a foam pith helmet, and then imagined Val D'Oro at that moment in all its grind and seasoned beauty. It and Rockfish were in the same game but they played with very different cards.

Tittle-tattling voices swirled around the balcony. There were locals and blow-ins, holidaying families and retired couples making second-bottle plans that deep down they knew they'd never see through. A Northumbrian apparently listed every chip shop he'd ever visited, and a woman with a West Midlands accent talked at length about her pub darts team. It felt like a long and contented afternoon somewhere on the continent, except with more references to Joan's ropey wrist and meat raffles. Big questions of class faded away. We were all fish and chips class, until our bills arrived at least.

My White Ling shared its plate with a lemon slice, a pickle curled up as if napping in a doorway and a cardboard gondola of tartare sauce. The chips had a metal bucket limousine of their own, divas who insisted on arriving separately. Rockfish offered them as 'unlimited', rekindling memories of my daughter's approach to 'bottomless' drinks on one particular visit to Nando's. There she'd consumed enough pop to burp so ferociously and sonorously that a woman on the next table blamed her husband and scolded him.

Swathed in a perfectly crumpled batter, the astonishing gold bullion of White Ling did not offer a flashback to other times, but a sensation of novelty. It felt important to realise that this uncomplicated delicacy could still feel new and different. The chips, with their melted-bath-duck-yellow hinds and tiny crispy stalagmites made me want to query whether 'unlimited' was a lifetime offer.

Beyond the balcony, the harbour water lightened and calmed almost to a standstill but for the odd furrowed ripple. It was punctured by a bald head above sparkling black eyes. A seal had caught a fair-sized fish and now feasted, slapping it around on the ocean surface. Garrotted and shredded, the fish's blood coloured the sea in the manner of a paint brush being dipped in a glass of water. 'Oh, how lovely!' cooed the West Midlands dart lady.

Overlooking the rear, oldest section of Brixham harbour is a monument to William of Orange. According to its dedication, he 'Landed near this spot' in 1688 and declared 'The liberties of England and the Protestant Religion I will maintain.' Today, an elderly man brushed pastry from his T-shirt onto the plinth and a seagull stood on William's disfigured head. He was watching – the seagull, that is – a mother and her two sons. They had opened an almighty cardboard box foraged from The Golden Fish, one of two chip shops opposite. The seagull was either contemplating a swoop on their loot or thinking, as I was, that their decision to submerge a battered fish in gravy could never, ever be justified. It was wrong in the Rhondda Valley, and it was wrong here. William of Orange, for once, said nothing.

As the family gathered around the box and plucked at its contents with wooden forks – a joyous scene, gravy or not – I thought about how the packaging of fish and chips was part of their charm. A server uprooting a box such as theirs and opening it in readiness for your order is moderately dramatic – here is the last moment before ownership is transferred and the adoption made. The spartan origami that goes into paper packaging is stagy too, and the arts and crafts feel of this off-white lining itself pleases. There are polystyrene trays that we engrave by accident with tiny forks, cones which siphon sauces and salt to the bottom, insulated paper bags for clutching tight on the way home. It is all part of the waiting and the theatre.

Now, much of that packaging carries variant designs based on newsprint with fake headlines and winning puns. The idea of wrapping our dish in newspaper also exists in a common idiom used by politicians or sportspeople keen to dismiss stories: 'Today's news is tomorrow's chip papers.' Here is a concept stored in the collective memory, and even held by some people who are unlikely to have experienced it

– at a memorable age anyhow – prior to its banning for reasons of hygiene in the 1980s.

Swaddling our chippy teas in column inches is, then, part of British folklore. For a long time, however, it was used to represent the earthy, working-class reputation of fish and chips. As Professor John K. Walton, a leading fish and chips academic, wrote in his excellent *Fish & Chips & The British Working Class, 1870–1940*: 'Eating out of newspaper, like eating in the street more generally, put forward a claim to unpretentiously democratic values and a spontaneity and informality that were widely prized in some kinds of working-class culture.'

Glyn Thomas, lyrical as ever, offered his own yarn: 'We as children when we got our chips in newspapers got the larger part of our culture, the larger part of our political education, from reading around the chip. We would actually delay over the eating of a chip because we were fascinated by the political comment made by the chap in the newspaper. And we would very often forsake a certain cooker of chips because he was taking the wrong paper.'

Newsprint or not, and everlasting Corbridge or Frinton snobbery aside, Professor Walton documented how fish and chips had, overall, been transformed from poor man's fodder reviled by the wealthy to an everyman institution. Though not necessarily in agreement, Walton highlighted an observation by the Lancastrian playwright Bill Naughton that: 'There was about fish and chips a sound democratic touch that no other food possessed; the poorest person could shop alongside the poshest ... You were all one in the kingdom of fish and chips.'

As we shall later see, during World War Two the fish and chips journey from pariah to national symbol accelerated. Across the sweep of the half century that followed, the chip shop leaned increasingly towards Naughton's democratic utopia. What remained steadfast was this food's reputation – it's *creed*, even – as being thoroughly proletarian and often northern. On television, for example, chippies were the preserve of *The Likely Lads* and *Last of the Summer Wine*. Even now, fish and chips shops are far more likely to be found in soapland than on tense dramas about people with kitchen islands and cleaners.

Where did Rockfish – and by extension Stein's – sit in all of this? Certainly, neither offered working-class prices if Blackpool was the barometer. Further, Rockfish was not necessarily *the* future of fish and chips, but *a* future. The Glasgow restaurant in the centre of town, the Oldham market café, the polished Rockfish; increasingly, my feeling was that there was room and customers for them all. Fish and chips did now cross social classes and erase boundaries, a great working-class gift to unity. And, notably, if with its £5 fish and chip Tuesdays Rockfish was recognising that this should never be an exclusive, unobtainable meal, then there was hope. Even a sailor down on his luck might just afford that, or a young dad without the gift of found money.

At the bus station in Brixham, I waited alongside two old ladies who began asking what had brought me to their dainty town. 'My mum used to call them "chips and fish"' said one of them. We all paused for a moment. 'It annoyed the hell out of me,' she concluded, waspishly. Brixham's church bells bonged and I departed for their brethren in Bow.

7.

CODS AND ROCKERS

London

'Fish and bread, a penny ...' they would holler and sing somewhere in between Amazon Fresh and Chilango Mexican restaurant. They echoed each other's words like gabbing magpies here on Chancery Lane and in the shadowy alleys and courtyards off it. From this part of town then down Leather Lane and all the way to Smithfield and Clerkenwell: 'Fish and bread, a penny ...'

It was the journalist Henry Mayhew who chronicled the fish fryers of London. From 1849 he set about recording the stories of those who lived and toiled in the city's dark corners and shabby trades. In the early 1860s his work was turned into a book, *London Labour and the London Poor*. It is an ink documentary of buyers and sellers, finders and pedlars, showmen and labourers.

There were, Mayhew reported, up to 350 such fryers oper-
ating. Most were men and boys, but more than 10 per cent
women and girls. Few of them were cooks or fishmongers
by trade, but instead mechanics, servants and those who
would turn their hand to anything if it almost paid for them
to be alive. Early each morning the fryers bought their fish
from the original Billingsgate Market; mainly plaice, sole,
haddock, whiting – whatever was cheapest. Back in their
Farringdon hovels, their harvest was washed, gutted,
squashed into small flat 'dabs' and then doused in flour and
water. This batter clenched the fish together and disguised
any ill odours. The dabs were fried for ten minutes in shallow
pans heated by fire barrows out in the street.

Then came the time for those mantra cries of 'Fish and
bread ...' Mayhew described how the fryers touted their
wares in two different ways. Some kept a street stall, usually
outside their home. This led to accusations that would soon
become familiar to the trade: that their work was a noxious
nuisance. 'The fried fish sellers live in some out-of-the-way
alley,' wrote Mayhew, 'and not infrequently in garrets, for
even among the poorest class there are great objections to
their being fellow lodgers on account of the odour from the
frying. Even when the fish is fresh (and it frequently is), the
odour is. rank.' He noted how their clothing was 'strongly
impregnated' with the smell, something they were blissfully
immune to.

Others were street wanderers, selling from 'a neatly
painted wooden tray, strung by a leathern strap from the

neck … the tray is papered over generally with newspapers, and on the paper is spread the shapeless brown lumps of fish'. Their takings came often from pubs and were bolstered at fairs and on race days down at Epsom.

In two habits suggesting a direct lineage to the fish we eat today, London fryers would garnish their offering with parsley and provide a salt box for customers to use at whatever volume pleased them. There was another precursor to a later trend – that of the many different terms used in chip shops around the country: what the sellers called 'dabs', the buyers knew as 'pieces'.

Mayhew interviewed a man in his late forties who had been hawking fried fish for seventeen years. Drifting around pubs with his tray, he had been confronted by pie-eyed, spiteful customers who ate, refused to pay and then responded to his pleas with their fists. On one occasion the fryer was temporarily blinded when a drinker threw black lead powder in his eyes. He believed that he had been targeted for dressing smartly compared to other sellers, continued Mayhew, some of whom wore 'white sleeves and apron' and others 'black calico sleeves and woollen aprons'.

Much of their London has been flattened and rebuilt. The more opulent state and status buildings of Holborn remain. In the shaded gloom these monoliths scatter beneath themselves like a gothic picnic blanket, the fish fryers can be imagined, hunched over their trackside infernos or toddling towards another pub. Their work took place in between public areas, hidden in half-spaces and hollow gaps, squalor nestled with grandeur. Purveyors of battered fish already knew where they belonged. Yet here it happened, their vapours gliding out from poverty and rubbing the noses of privilege. On an opulent wall near Old Square I encountered a peeling, gnawed wooden sign that may well still carry hints of haddock or sole. 'The Porters & Police have orders to remove all Persons making a Noise,' it said. Knowing their aromas could not be so easily tamed must have pleased the more rebellious fryers, something of a legal technicality among the highest courts.

Walking by legal types in their neckerchiefs and capes, I passed a bar offering cocktails and pétanque and muttered 'Bloody London' to myself as northerners are morally obliged to do. Nearby was Ye Olde Cock Tavern, a narrow, hemmed-in building bringing to mind a kid squeezed between two larger others in a school photo, and the kind of pub our fryers lived from and possibly for. I continued to Fetter Lane, moneyed from the surface up, but tarred in fishy cooking oil deep below. Leather Lane Market had just finished and its stallholders had departed. Perhaps trying to fancy dress the street in the uniform of its Victorian fish-frying self, they had left behind oil vat debris and a vague stench of death.

Before Mayhew wrote of this area's fish trading, Charles Dickens did. In *Oliver Twist*, serialised between 1837 and 1839 by *Bentley's Miscellany*, Fagin's den is close to Field Lane with its 'fried-fish warehouse'. Dickens also wrote of how 'Hunger was shred into atomics in every farthing porringer of husky chips of potato, fried with some reluctant drops of oil,' in *A*

Tale of Two Cities, published in 1859. That scene took place in Paris. Dickens was yet to match fish with chips but clearly knew of both individually.

Near to Herbal Hill, appealing scents broke free from a Vietnamese restaurant and decorated the air. As the population changes, so too do the perfumes of our pavements. One of Mayhew's fryers landing here today would have been disorientated by such unfamiliar aromas.

Field Lane is now gone. It trickled from Saffron Hill, still here though stacked with almighty office blocks. I walked its claustrophobic length, shady and dimmed, as if modelled on a dense pine forest. It released me opposite the rotting carcass of Smithfield Market, no doubt known to Mayhew's men and their penny sales. They, though, were not the first Londoners to fry fish.

The DLR train fluttered past the modern Billingsgate Market. Much of the catch sold there early that morning had already been battered and devoured. At Poplar, a flock of students boarded. One read to the others from his phone. 'Here's a good one. How many time zones are there in Russia?' This question was followed by several more. On each occasion, one particular teenage lad would answer: 'London?' Finally, as we approached Bow Church, his big moment came. 'Where were the 2012 Olympics held?' posed the quizmaster. Those of us in earshot silently willed him on. I even prepared a cheer. 'Rome?' he replied.

The Tube from Bow Road shrieked and then stopped abruptly. Everyone sat in silence listening to a woman crunch Kettle Chips, a very British torture method. The carriage seemed to sneeze itself back into life, whistle its way to boiling point like an old kettle and then simmer into Stepney Green.

Somewhere beneath today's East End bus lanes and tower blocks, sixteenth-century Jewish immigrants fried battered fish. They had brought the delicacy – sizzled on meatless Fridays and eaten cold through Shabbat – here from their native Portugal. This introduction is detailed in *The Book of Jewish Food* by Claudia Roden, who also writes how, following a visit to London, President Thomas Jefferson reported that he had eaten 'fish in the Jewish fashion'.

With chipped potatoes most likely a French or Belgian invention, our national dish, then, has resolutely foreign origins. When Professor Panikos Panayi, author of *Fish & Chips: A Takeaway History*, became one of the first academics to highlight this truth in another of his books, *Spicing Up Britain*, he faced patriotic opposition and was even included on the 'Know Your Enemy' section of a neo-Nazi website. In *Fish & Chips*, Panayi details how Jewish people in London were selling their fried fish even prior to Mayhew's subjects, many of whom were likely Jewish. By the 1920s, he demonstrates, one in five London chippies were owned by Jewish families. Notably, the author also catalogues some of the toxic and persistent antisemitism Jewish fryers faced through the decades. Like the Italians, they were well acquainted with Alien status and the slurs it provoked.

On Mile End Road, statues of Caroline and William Booth face each other. William's raised arm and pointed finger makes it appear as if he is performing the Bee Gees' *Stayin' Alive* in a perpetual dance-off with Caroline, his wife. She looks entirely nonplussed, and as if none of his moves are new.

Closer inspection revealed that these likenesses commemorated the Booths' founding of the Salvation Army, and its helping of the East End poor. The couple's work was a response to poverty. So, inadvertently, was the rise of fish and chip shops throughout this locale of hungry streets. A cheap, filling meal could in its own way change lives and lift spirits.

A tall brick archway resembling a Lego figure's trousers announced that I had reached Globe Town, an enclave of Tower Hamlets. Opposite, a property developer measured up outside The Carpenter's Arms, a pub built into a tower block and probably referred to as 'a proper boozer' by locals of a certain vintage. I sat on a feeble, teetering bench by the Lego trousers and enjoyed the melodies of various languages sailing over garden fences. Three pigeons disputed custody of a fag end and a council worker swept the ground around an empty statue plinth. It was once graced by a fountain sculpture, *Woman & Fish* by Frank Dobson, removed after repeated vandalising. This neglected square on Cephas Road was named after him, and it was also the spot where fish and chips were probably invented.

The Malin family were Jewish immigrants who lived at 78 Cleveland Way. Though half of the old street remains, their section was bulldozed to make way for Frank Dobson Square and the parade of shops which accompanies it. The parent Malins' trade was rug weaving, but the family also sold hot chipped potatoes on the streets of Bow and Bethnal Green. One day in 1860 or thereabouts, son Joseph Malin, not long a teenager, bought battered fish from a nearby shop. Back home, the boy paired it with a portion of his family's chips. Unbeknownst to him, he had given birth to a culinary icon. 78 Cleveland Way was later – possibly in 1865 – transformed into the country's very first chippy. Or so goes the legend.

The dates are sketchy, the details scarce. Some have claimed that Malin chips were circular and so did not count. Mr Barlow would certainly not have agreed with this telling of the fish and chips story. A leap of faith has to be taken, a belief in mythology. Perhaps that much is fitting for this fabled dish and its neon houses. Certainly, by the late 1960s, the NFFF was on board with one interpretation of the Malin account. In 1968 they raised a plaque above the fish and chip shop of Joseph Malin's descendants, at 560 Old Ford Road. It marked 'The World's Oldest Fish and Chip Business' and '100 Years of Fish of Chips'.

The plaque had been handed to Malin's great-great-grandson during a ceremonial dinner at a salubrious London hotel. A government minister hailed 'This landmark in British eating habits', and the NFFF chairman saluted a 'Very important and history-making day'. Not everyone could hear them: a Lancastrian rebel heckled throughout, bawling that Lee's of Mossley was Britain's first and oldest. '1863! 1863!' came the cries. I have been unable to verify Mr Barlow's where-abouts that afternoon in 1968.

As Joseph Malin helped cultivate the family shop, a slightly younger Jewish immigrant was growing up in neighbouring Whitechapel. Samuel Isaacs was born in 1856 and in child-hood helped his father, known as Mo Fisher, sell fried fish from a cart pulled by a donkey. East End lore clung to Mo Fisher long after he had passed away; many said that he was the first man in Britain to sell fried fish, perhaps a chronolog-ical stretch.

When his son turned 18, Mo gifted him a small fish and chip shop in Lambeth. Sam worked devilishly hard, wheel-barrowing his supplies from Billingsgate every morning. At 21, he had a key to the door of a second chippy. More followed until, in 1896, he opened London's first fish and chip restaurant, in Shoreditch. Never had the East End work-ing class been served their sole and chips by waiting staff, or on plates. Nine pence bought them their meal with bread and butter, a cup of tea and the rare feeling of princely priv-ilege. Their love for the Isaacs way of doing things was infectious. Sam had created a trend. The number of restau-rants opening multiplied, a rare chain in a trade that has always tended more towards its independent republics. By the time he died in 1939, aged 83, there were twenty-two Isaacs fish and chips restaurants in the capital and beyond.

Back on the segment of Cleveland Way that the wrecking ball missed, shopkeepers smoked in doorways and an old lady with eyes wiser than time fanned herself with the hood of her sari. I turned my back on them, and on Frank Dobson Square, and continued to Bethnal Green. Here, the aristocrat Baroness Angela Burdett-Coutts had begun Columbia Street Market with her husband, William, owner of a North Sea fishing fleet. According to Pierre Picton, the Baroness could also be the person who first betrothed fish with chips.

While touring the world as the wealthy did, Burdett-Coutts had apparently witnessed the Italian way of frying potato slices, then tried it here and paired the dish with fried fish. Writer Keith Waterhouse, in a romantic essay about fish and chips for the *Daily Mail*, repeated the Baroness theory: 'A noted philanthropist called Baroness Angela Burdett-Coutts, of the banking family, is credited with bringing fish and chips together – presumably in the interests of nourishing the deserving poor, since I cannot imagine she saw fish as something to serve up to the Rothschilds next time they came to dinner.'

I could find no further trace of this story, though did learn that Westminster Abbey buried Burdett-Coutts' coffin vertically due to what we might now call 'an administrative error'.

I walked onwards, suddenly obsessed with seeing the 1968 Malin plaque on Old Ford Road. Although we are living through an age of righteous, and often justified, attacks on controversial statues and memorials, the thought of daubing it with pro-Lees graffiti on behalf of the North only fleetingly crossed my mind. Not that I was short on time to reflect. Number 560 was, I calculated, at the far end of Old Ford Road which meant an interminable trek that should really have seen me rewarded with the Duke of Edinburgh medal I missed out on at school (largely through never signing up). Finally, just short of the Olympic Stadium, I reached my destination. The plaque had been removed.

There is a detailed sketch in a 1911 edition of the *Illustrated London News* that depicts a chaotic scene in a fish and chip shop. 'In Foreign London,' reads the caption, 'Where Aliens Much Do Congregate.' Accompanying text avows how 'In the East-End more especially' fish and chips has 'a certain place. The alien population there welcome it most,' but chippies are also 'favoured by men, women, and children of the humbler classes, who find it a great convenience, for they can purchase it, at a cost of ha'pence'. 'All sorts and conditions of poor are seen,' eating or 'More often, taking them home in a piece of newspaper.'

The feature is vaguely patronising, possibly antisemitic and certainly xenophobic. Yet a rather more positive, alternative conclusion can be drawn: that, three years before ghastly World War, fish and chips had the power to unite people of many backgrounds. This unity may have been forged from necessity – all of those mentioned shared the characteristics of being poor and finding affordable sustenance in the chippy. Yet it remains valid to highlight this early evidence of chip shop democracy.

The insinuation of East End 'Aliens' certainly included Jewish people, and an accurate image would have included Italians, both as customers and proprietors. The latter, while not featuring on the scale they did in Scotland, were a significant presence.

A later illustration may also have included Greek Cypriots. Professor Panayi, himself born in London to Greek Cypriot parents, demonstrated the immense influence of his Mediterranean compatriots on the trade after they started to arrive in large numbers from the 1950s. Most hailed from Cyprus' rural areas but they settled primarily in London. By 1975, Panayi shows, at least 150 out of 800 capital fish and chips shops were Greek Cypriot-owned. Soon, successful Cypriots were opening shops throughout the country.

London's oldest surviving fish and chip shop has been under the stewardship of the Cypriot Ziyaeddin family since 1980. The Rock & Sole Plaice, a haven between berserk Covent Garden and teeming Theatreland, was established in 1871 under a less punning name lost to time. For the barrow boys and factory workers who became customers, this scented intruder must have seemed emphatically novel, a true curiosity shop. Seventy years on, and by then a restaurant too, it became the headquarters for an operation to feed locals left homeless by Nazi bomb raids.

From the 1920s until the late 1960s, the shop was owned by Ray Fenner, grandson of its founder. His daughters, Anna and Rachel, still lived above it when the Ziyaeddins took over. A board of frilly words on today's shop front salutes the role of 'The Three Pillars' – Anna, Rachel and Mary Goody. The latter had worked in the shop during the 1910s and 1920s and, reads the inscription, was 'matriarch of the area and the first to point out that as the new owners of the Rock & Sole, we were not good enough'. Together they schooled the Ziyaeddins in how to prepare and cook fish and chips precisely as they had been prepared and cooked on this London corner since 1871.

By the time he spoke to the *Observer* magazine in 2006, patriarch Hassan Ziyaeddin was a master of the frying range and a pillar of the community himself. His tale was an encore of many Italians' experience in Scotland – arriving as a novice, working prodigiously to become a success and along the way leaning into the gritty romance of the trade. He might just have struck up a friendship with our Rhondda Valley poet Gwyn Thomas should the two have met. 'The week I arrived in London from Cyprus in 1960,' he explained, 'I had fish and chips for the first time, wrapped in newspaper. Anyone under 30 does not remember that people found and read stories this way.' He also offered a poetic summary of a frying hazard: 'Sometimes I see a splash of oil coming up into the air and it heads directly into the eye, as if in slow motion. You can see it coming but are mesmerised by the reflection.'

Cream and green-fronted and spreading onto Endell Street with a canopied outdoor seating area, The Rock & Sole Plaice appears like some Parisian neighbourhood brasserie. Fittingly, a table of four French visitors were sitting beneath the awning now. One held up a capsule of mushy peas and inspected it with the fervour of a jeweller viewing a diamond through a loupe. Beyond them by the kerb laid a jumble of empty polystyrene ice boxes, which from afar had resembled a melting snowman. The top trunk's label disclosed that it had arrived from 'J Nash, Billingsgate' and had contained large dogfish supplied from Grimsby. 'Rock' was scrawled beneath the label – rarely in chippies has dogfish been referred to by its actual name, possibly because it conjures images of an animal happily playing fetch at the beach one morning before being snared by a trawler net.

Passing wall pillars marked 'Anna', 'Rachel' and 'Mary', a waiter escorted me to a far corner table. There was a brilliant, crisp lightness to this room encased as it was by two walls of long windows and dressed in white tiles. Simon & Garfunkel's 'Sound of Silence' played and it felt like a wedding venue before the guests have arrived. Across those windows were half a dozen repeats of the restaurant logo. In this version of the Blackpool chef's hat cod, the fish wore a top hat and held in its fin a cane, as if it had swum to London and become gentrified.

Up at the counter, a young customer responded to the salt and vinegar question by joining his hands as if in prayer before pleading: 'You just cannot put enough on, mate.' 'But none for me,' interjected the suited old man who was next in the queue. 'He can have mine!' There were several tables of American people, including three women in their early twenties posing for selfies with their fish and chips, an awkward manoeuvre that risked unwelcome intimacy with their plastic tubs of tartare sauce. 'I feel like we should just ask someone to take a photo,' said one of them before continuing with her selfie.

Next to me, a lone diner moved her head incrementally towards the plate as if in some delicate worship ritual. Once she had made eye contact with her chips, she shot backwards suddenly, frightening the life out of me like a suddenly protruding Ghost Train skeleton. Across the way, a customer ordered the pitta bread starter 'Because I am Greek,' and his partner carved the white fish from its batter, leaving a golden slipper on her plate.

With an offer of cod, haddock, rock, plaice, lemon sole or skate, the menu was testament to the tradition of southern chippies offering more variety of fish. A sign above the range proclaimed that they fried in groundnut oil – no dripping here. Marvellously, The Rock and Sole Plaice raised the prospect of peace between north and south by offering both 'London-style Sides' (homemade coleslaw, gherkins, pickled onion and pickled egg) and 'Northern Style Sides' (curry sauce, gravy, mushy peas). That the northerners were 50p cheaper was immensely gratifying.

It was not a surprise to see skate on the menu. 'If skate's not on the menu it's a good rule of thumb to go to another fish-and-chip shop,' Hassan Ziyaeddin had pronounced when speaking to the *Observer*, 'because skate's the fish which shows a fryer's real mettle. If it's cooked right, it's the most beautiful thing. But if it's only cooked 90 per cent it'll put someone off skate for the rest of their life.' Ziyaeddin's successors showed their mettle now, engrossed as they were in dunking and dropping, checking and scooping. One wore a white catering trilby and altered dials on the range control, soft engineering to render those skate and cod into perfection.

In 2010, batter expert Peter Hill had told BBC Radio Four of different regional preferences across Britain. In Scotland they liked flat, rippled batters. Yorkshire and Lancashire were united by their penchant for something harder and with the crispness of a Cadbury's Crunchie bar. In the Midlands a crunch was appreciated but their favourite batters could be compared more to spiky sheets. Londoners agreed with the Scots on flatness but desired something crispier.

Perhaps once more channelling their conciliatory approach, the friers of The Rock and Sole Plaice had conjured a batter that seemed to be all of these things. In an almost lustrous streetlight shade, it varied from tip to tail, an edible map. When I applied salt it gushed out violently, submerging the flat Caledonian uplands in ash. It didn't help that my concentration had been robbed by the chips: the glorious, broad chips. Many were perhaps twice the width of standard chippy offerings, beams instead of bollards. They occupied one half of the oval plate like railway sleepers dropped from the sky.

Here were truly original, *different* fish and chips. A method of cooking had been transmitted through 150 years so that on the plate now were the products of a Victorian worker's creativity. This was time travel eating. Mayhew's fryers may well have recognised at least half of the meal I was about to eat. London: the city where everything changes but the chips stay the same.

8.

THE DRIPPING FORECAST

Bradford and Leeds

'Today's going too fast,' said the teenage girl to her dad. 'This whole week has.' He nodded and a few seconds lapsed. 'Very true, love,' came the reply, 'and try being my bloody age.' We all stood looking at the Underground map in that doe-eyed, half-bamboozled manner that visitors do. I was ready to hit the North, but only after lunch.

Oxford Street was restless as ever, a crucible of ill-tempers and discombobulated tourists. A man wearing a sandwich board was tangled in the parade. 'The End is Nigh,' it claimed, as it has been for many years. I turned right onto Poland Street, which awarded the sudden calm of diving underwater. 'Fish & Chips' flagged the red and white sign, beckoning the passerby lustily. It was the very antithesis of apocalyptic tidings; hope over doom.

Golden Union restaurant rained the instant feeling of spare and sainted time, as if the school bell had sounded. A teenage boy offered hearty greetings from beneath a menu list whose prices were lit in small neon boxes, lending it the air of a scoreboard. Pickled onions, gherkins and eggs were accompanied by a plant-based offering. Here was another vision of the chippy future. There was even a free jukebox.

Customers shellshocked to be liberated from the Oxford Circus melodrama queued between the chrome promise of the frying range and a wall coated with a strident tile mural of three magical words: Fish and Chips. My seat faced the frying range and counter, from where waiting staff monitored tables with the vigilance of deep-end lifeguards.

Golden Union radiated a joyous mood. In appearance it was not unlike an American diner, but with the welcome cloy of tangy vinegar. In the short gaps between jukebox offerings, pans hummed bubbling B-sides and staff giggled through jokes only they knew. It felt like a holiday place, a parcel of seaside majesty transplanted. Soon, brittle batter and soothing chips threw me to another world as if my plate was telling a story.

As she collected my ransacked crockery the Golden Union co-owner, Kerry, saw my stuffed and swollen rucksack and asked for where I was bound. In replying, I mentioned my instant affection for her restaurant. 'From a northerner, that's a real compliment,' she smiled. I also expressed my pathetic sadness that scraps seemed impossible to find in the south of England. 'We've got scraps, if you ask!' she replied. 'I should put on the menu: "You can ask for scraps." We do scraps, we do gravy, and we do curry sauce, and we do mushy peas.'

We talked about other north/south chippy divides, and the London way of frying in oil rather that dripping. Golden Union had lived now for sixteen years, despite its fresh demeanour, and in the early days they fried in duck fat. Then tastes and sensitivities changed. 'If I had my way,' concluded Kerry, 'we'd have a separate pan. We could have Dripping Tuesdays!' Departing, I said my farewells. 'Enjoy Yorkshire,' said Kerry. 'We'll make sure we give you scraps next time you're down.'

Rolling out of King's Cross, I thought about the differences between chippies in my part of England and the capital. The dripping versus oil schism seems to have rumbled on for quite some time. In that lovelorn essay, Keith Waterhouse wrote of his 1930s Leeds childhood, 'The chippy at the top of the hill used pure beef dripping while the chippie at the bottom of the hill was reputed to use southern muck like sunflower oil, equated in our part of the world with brake fluid.'

Waterhouse's sentiments expressed a prejudice many of us northerners comfortably wallow in: that fish and chips are somehow *ours*. An element of this idea is that the true, proper frying matter is dripping. As southern chippies shy away from deploying it, they are regarded as faint imitators. We are the grittier, earthier people and we own the national dish. This, of course, disregards those many shops beneath, say, Sheffield that do use dripping, and ditto northern oil merchants, a growing band. Yet this story is one of myth and mystique and feeling over fact. Gerald Priestland knew that much. 'Fish & chips are still very widely regarded as wearing a cloth cap and being wrapped in the *News of the World*,' he wrote. 'Quite affluent northerners are still convinced that they are part of an essentially working-class way of life; while southerners who are often no better off still regard them as "not for us", as if they were some kind of charity relief for the poor.'

Another BBC short film, from 1970, sharply echoed this theme. Citizens of Bury were pitted against a southern housewife who had been affronted by their eating habits during a Lancastrian spell. 'Up north, people used to think I was a bit mad,' she explains, 'because I did so much cooking. They could send their children to the fish and chip shop and get pie, chips and peas for a couple of bob and that was their dinner.' One northern riposte came from a woman who labelled southerners 'Snobbish ... They don't eat enough chips.' 'I eat them about twice a week,' continued another from her newsagent workplace. 'This is because we're busy. A lot of people in the north also don't like the idea of people in the south. They're snobs. I haven't been down south, but from what customers have told me, they wouldn't like to live there.'

In the late eighties market research by Mintel included fish and chips in its evidence of the ever-broadening gap between England's two halves. 'The South-east,' said research director Frank Fletcher, 'is already out of step with the rest of the country in both social and economic terms. Northerners eat fish and chips, cakes and soups, while southerners eat a cosmopolitan mixture of food.' At the same time, National Federation of Fish Friers general secretary Arthur Parrington brought the issue of skin into the equation, commenting: 'The southerners are perhaps a bit more barbaric with their fish and chips whereas in the north we have connoisseurs. If I tried frying fish with its skin on, I would lose my own skin.'

Slings and arrows were not launched solely from the northern side. In 1997, when the West Yorkshire fish and chip chain Harry Ramsden's opened a branch in Oxford, restaurant critic for the *Oxford Mail* Chris Gray lamented, 'How out of tune it all seems in a sophisticated, cosmopolitan city like Oxford. Palates more used to balsamic vinegar are bluntly offered Sarson's. Drinkers of Earl Grey and Lapsang get only Yorkshire Tea. Folk who might agonise between demi-glace or chasseur sauce must settle for Bisto onion gravy.'

There is a border – possibly running through the brewery town of Tadcaster – where the fish and chip shops of my native North Yorkshire become the 'Fisheries' of West Yorkshire. As the bus picked its way through the outskirts of Leeds, I noticed several of them: Key Fisheries in Seacroft with its giant yellow proclamation of 'HADDOCK' in one window, a reminder of this area's devotion to that species over cod; redbrick York Road Fisheries where a customer showed his bag of chips to someone on the receiving end of a video call; Famous Golden Fisheries and its sign on which a haddock seemed to be trying to eat an ampersand.

That morning, the bus had been so late that it induced in those waiting a mild and passing madness. One man kicked stones at a drain on the opposite side of the road and gave out a loud cheer if one plopped through the grate. The woman with him intensively examined the temporary road maintenance markings in front of us before turning and offering: '"Gas," that one says. That must be where the gas is.' Then an elderly gentleman, bald but for a u-shaped slab of hair around the back and sides, began ferociously combing the vacant sheen of his crown. I began to wonder whether we had been waiting for such a long time that he had unknowingly gone bald.

After a change in Leeds, I set out for Bradford. The city has always prompted thoughts of fish and chips. Being taken to the original Harry Ramsden's restaurant in the nearby town of Guiseley was an occasional childhood treat. First, we would visit the wooden hut where Ramsden had first produced fish and chips. Then came a promising, if long, queue including more shuffling pensioners than I had ever seen in one place, until finally we walked beneath the chandeliers and to our table. The Harry Ramsden's brand was eventually floated on the stock market as a chain exporting their solid yet flamboyant northern ways across this country and beyond. The figure of Ramsden himself was often emphasised, a kind of KFC Colonel of the West Riding. This over-expansion resulted, ultimately, in closures and several venture capital buy-outs. The original Harry Ramsden's is now part of the Wetherby Whaler chain, and the hut has been demolished owing to asbestos. Perhaps the ghost of Harry loiters in the car park like a deposed king, shaking his head in despair over a palace lost.

The Bradford bus skirted close to a chip shop 9 miles from Ramsden's and founded five years later, in 1933. The pans still rumble at Ritz Fisheries, which has outlived its opulent neighbour. The Ritz's 'warm shabbiness' featured in a 1970 book called *Nation of Shopkeepers* by Greville Havenhand. 'It only sells one sort of fish – haddock,' he wrote. 'The people in that part of Yorkshire are conservative. They like haddock and they like it fried in dripping.' Havenhand explained how the 'cheerful Leeds United supporter' in charge of the Ritz analysed television listings to guess when customer numbers would climb and drop and enjoyed his own creations: 'I eat them once or twice a day.'

Professor John K. Walton showed how Bradford's association with fish and chips predates Harry Ramsden's. In 1914, the city boasted at least 317 chippies, one for every 1,000 residents. There was even a council-appointed inspector of fried fish shops, and a fish and chip shop permit for each new housing estate was embedded in local planning rules.

More recently, in 1999, citizens showed their fierce loyalty to local chip shops when a dastardly southern interloper wrote a letter to the *Bradford Telegraph & Argus*. He claimed: 'It's a myth that northern fish and chips are the best. Most fish and chips I've had in Bradford have been disgusting, with pale undercooked chips that are swimming in grease, with fish that is usually grey and tasteless on the inside and batter that either tastes like wallpaper paste or is as hard as concrete.' Incensed replies flowed. 'Of course, northern fish and chips are better than those in the south! Where are the most fish and chip shops? In the north. Where are the most fish and chips eaten? In the north,' said one correspondent. 'There's nothing wrong with our fish and chips. We're quite happy with what we produce,' added another.

Down by Centenary Square, locals gathered their bundles from The In Plaice and unfurled them beneath epic Bradford Town Hall. The blackboard advertised today's 'Fish butty and pop' special deal. Even without going inside, I knew that those pops would be proper chippy varieties of the type seldom seen elsewhere: my Dandelion and Burdock or Vimto of course, but also Sunkist and Tizer, and perhaps even American Cream Soda or Bitter Shandy. This lesser-spotted tin kaleidoscope lends a chip shop drinks fridge the allure of a foreign supermarket.

Walking through Bradford's blend of Victorian frills and Brutalist temples is always transfixing, as if you are watching two different films at once. This was especially true today, however, because terrific sunshine rendered the city's grand old limestone buildings ice pop-luminous and its seventies concrete titans galactic. I hauled myself up Lumb Lane, where civic Bradford fades and hollow mills cling to scrubland. One colossal worsted wool works chimney soared ahead, a silent poem about what this place once was.

At number 118, between sari shops and curry houses, is Mirza Travel, specialists in packages for the Muslim Hajj and Umrah pilgrimages. Their carpet masks a shrine to fish and chips, if we believe another version of the origin narrative. In that telling it was here, just as Malin and Lees were frying for the first time, that seventeen-year-old Clara Duce began doing the same.

118 Lumb Lane was the Duce family's grocery store and Clara introduced the sale of fish and chips here as a side product. She may even have been the first to pair them. Opposite the property are iron gates to nowhere, the mill that once churned and threshed here having been erased. Yet it is possible to imagine its workers swelling out before the shift end hooter had even finished bellowing, drawn in by the scent of frying food. The idea of this uncommon new treat must have made exhausting shifts move along a little quicker.

Clara Duce is also a pacifying figure in the north/south divide side story of our national dish. A Hertfordshire girl by birth, she continued in the chippy trade, opening a small band of shops in Bradford. Then, in the 1880s, she and her growing family – soon to include ten children – returned south. They opened more fish and chip shops across the

Home Counties, perhaps missionaries for the northern way of frying. The business bloomed into an assortment of much-loved chippies, handed down through the generations. Duces still own chip shops now.

Clara Duce, the first lady of fish and chips, passed away in 1933. There is plenty of room in the field opposite the shop. A statue would fit perfectly.

The Bradford fryers were restless. They and their comrades across the country believed that the fish and chip industry should be deemed an essential trade for the duration of World War One. That way, ingredient and oil supplies could flow and the working class would not go hungry. Sensing his members' fury, National Federation of Fish Friers president John Pullan threatened the government, warning that if help did not arrive, 'Then it could look out for trouble.' Notably, concessions were made by panicked ministers.

The principal chronicler of this wrangle is Professor Walton. In his book *Fish & Chips & The British Working Class*, he revealed how many within the trade – and perhaps even in government – believed that the continued availability of the dish prevented a starving people rebelling, as had happened in Germany and Russia. 'Now the war is over,' contended the Northern Counties Federation of Fish Fryers in 1919, 'Government interest is dead. We have served their purpose, keeping off hunger, stemming revolution.' Further, wrote Walton, there grew a 'widespread and enduring notion among fryers' that fish and chips had 'played a crucial part in winning the war by keeping the munitions workers fed and sustaining their morale'.

Perhaps the terror of a Fish and Chip Revolution lingered into World War Two. From 1940, chip shops were no longer considered an Offensive Trade, and were given exemptions to rationing and subsidies so that they could continue to serve. That same year of 1940 saw a meeting in which new Prime Minister Winston Churchill was warned by Ernest Bevin that the morale of northern shipyard and munitions workers had been undermined by fish and chip shortages. *The Scotsman* concurred, arguing 'It would have been unthinkable that the chip should have suffered in a war for democracy, for chips are of the essence of democracy,' and 'When the full history of the war comes to be written we hope that due tribute to the chip will be paid as one of our greatest morale builders.' Some years later, a newspaper letter writer named Ivor Brown remembered how that early period of scarcity owing to fat shortage 'was for Britain one of the major horrors of war'.

Churchill understood the importance of fish and chips to the country's mood and the propaganda value of a dish he called the 'Happy Companions' in a 1943 House of Commons debate. Perhaps his time as an MP in Edward de Gernier's Dundee and then the Oldham of Dandy and Mr Dyson had been influential.

Strategies for the continuing supply of fish and chips after Nazi invasion were also drafted. In 1941 the NFFF confirmed that its 23,000 members would be available in the event of significant air attack. They would continue to fry and could obtain emergency supplies of fat. Three years later, a stark *Western Daily Press* headline read simply: 'Invasion: Fish and Chips,' before accounting for NFFF and Government plans. 'Fish fryers anticipating a possible upsetting of transport arrangements when the invasion starts,' began the story, 'are taking steps to ensure that the public will get their fish and chips.'

As in 1918, there was from 1945 an acknowledgement that fish and chips had contributed enormously to the war effort. Chippies had played a symbolic role, bolstering the national mood through bleak times. And they had fulfilled a physical one, keeping workers well fed for a few pence. I just wish I'd asked my grandad what that first chippy tea back home after wartime service was like. Even demobbed and gung ho after having survived a kamikaze attack, mind, he still wouldn't have eaten fish with the skin on.

Grandad was a Loiner – the local term for a native of Leeds seldom used outside the city – and I thought of him while returning to his home city from Bradford. The bus driver had been spectacularly sarcastic to a passenger who'd failed to return his friendly greeting, leaning out and barking down the gangway, 'Oh well you seem right nice, you do, flower.' Both of my grandads were Leeds bus drivers, and it was an exchange the skin-off version would have relished. I recalled now that he'd once been in a chip shop queue when a woman he regarded as 'a batty old sod' had entered and said, 'I think I've just seen a cuckoo.' Grandad turned and announced, 'I think *you're* a bit bloody cuckoo, love.'

Gerald Priestland called Leeds the 'intellectual capital' of fish and chips, given that the NFFF – so vital in those years of conflict – was, and still is, based here. Now, among other services, they run a week-long course in which would-be fryers learn the art and science of cooking fine products and running a shop. If Leeds is a chippy capital, then Keith Waterhouse must have been its laureate. This segment of his essay is best imagined in the voice of Sean Bean or Jodie Whittaker, Dvorak's *New World Symphony* sweeping away in the background: 'It is a delicacy that goes with distant tram-cars clanging through the fog, with closing time and the aftertaste of Best Bitter and Woodbine smoke, with the rush out of the two-and-nines before the first revved-up tinny notes of the National Anthem could turn you into stone and put you 20 places behind in the queue outside the next-door chippy. It goes with families crowded round the kitchen table, enjoying an unexpected late supper bonus because Pa was feeling peckish. Togetherness. This is nation's heritage stuff we are talking here.'

Like Pa, I was now peckish. Straying through the immense Kirkgate Market, as ever a world of its own, I bought some Midget Gems from the same stall I always had, a paper bag dessert for later. 'We Buy Owt' bellowed a placard attached to a motley bric-à-brac stall as unseen voices chanted of cheap punnets and discount bananas. The market has long had a chip shop, now called The Fisherman's Wife. I had already chosen, though, to rove upwards into the suburbs and Oakwood Fish Bar, a haunt of my parents' during those heady days of The Beatles and beehives.

The teenage couple sitting behind me on the bus to Oakwood were having separate conversations. It was useful practice for any potential marriage. 'Just me and 90,000 goths in a field, imagine it,' and 'Why do sign makers' shops always have such crap signs?' were both promising topic leads, but the pair alighted at Sheepscar, ready to ignore each other in a different part of town. They were replaced by two students who discussed historical events in a breezy, gossipy manner – 'So Zhukov goes to Stalin, and he's like, "I totally need more tanks", and Stalin's like …'

We thundered through Harehills and its redbrick rows with lines of washing suspended between upstairs windows like tightropes clad in underwear. At Oakwood, houses spread out and changed from brick to stone. Families bound for lush Roundhay Park bought deli picnics and there was mention of a fête. Chip shop fragrances of vinegar and blistering batter glided on the warm summer air. I crossed a road, heading for the circular window.

Much of the beauty possessed by the chippies encountered during my travels was, admittedly, often in the eye that beheld them. Yet Oakwood Fish Bar is objectively stunning. More than half of its square, gleaming-black Art Deco front is occupied by a circular window with silver grilles. My parents recalled a 'Frying Tonight' sign flashing at its centre in the 1960s. Above it, artful red letters declare FISH BAR, with geometric lines forking down towards the round-windowed double door. It looks as if a giant vinyl record has been placed over the brickwork of a moody old West Yorkshire sandstone building. Even without the entrancing scents that now escaped each time the doors flapped open, it would have been impossible to walk by.

Inside, Formica symmetry was a calming throwback to another, slower point in time. Since 1934, customers have been ordering at the chrome counter with its condiment and pickle regiment, and then turning to wait while watching the world through a circle. 'Registered Member,' attested an antique oval plaque in this city's civic yellow and purple shades, 'Leeds & District Fish Friers' Association.' A friendly lad in his late teens waved over from behind the Leeds-built Spitfire frying range. 'Be with you in a second, mate.'

Wishing to recreate a childhood classic, I ordered chips, a bread roll and some bits, as scraps are known to some here and in other parts of Yorkshire. 'How I love fish and chips,' sings John Shuttleworth from 40 miles down the road in Sheffield, 'With mushy peas and those battery bits / That some call bits and some call scraps.' In our house, the Scrap Butty was an hors d'oeuvre fashioned from one slice of buttered white bread sprinkled with scraps and rolled into a delightful duvet. This hallowed item could be rapidly snaffled while main meals were slid onto plates and ketchup bottles shaken loose. When its spongy core gave way to a batter crunch, it invoked the guilty thrill of throwing Fun Snaps in the dark.

The Oakwood's teenage fryer made me realise once more how a good chippy stands on the shoulders of its staff. Knowledgeable and impassioned, he had the air of an enthused hobbyist rather than someone for whom this was merely a weekend pocket money job. Checking on pans and turning fish, he was another to talk of how difficult running a chippy had become, even if a near-tripling of the price of potatoes was not his cross to bear. That burden fell to owner Steven, busying around in the back, who according to the teenager 'Probably served your parents.' The teenager was displeased by the shop's latest batch of spuds, though felt they were making for 'decent enough chips. I'll do you a good portion. I like to give good portions.' He spoke too of the struggle to compete with a well-resourced local rival, although he felt the Oakwood had a crucial taste advantage: 'We fry in dripping. They don't.'

At the outdoor tables beneath the circle, I sat and unwound my smouldering wrappers, deploying a can of Dandelion and Burdock as an ever-decreasing paperweight. Scraps snowed onto bread and I bit into my childhood. Along from me, a woman in her eighties looked perturbed and preoccupied. Then, a middle-aged man strutted from the doorway, two white packages held tight like charity collection boxes. She looked up to him, suddenly Oliver Twist in front of the gruel kitchen master, and asked: 'Did ... Did they have bits?' Taking a seat, he looked across. Whole years of fondness danced across his eyes. 'Yes, Mam. They had bits.' She smiled as if a bad time had ended.

9.

TAIL END

Stamford Bridge, Whitby and South Shields

Crossing into the East Riding, a girl of 15 or 16 was complaining about the train shenanigans that had accounted for her taking this bus instead. 'So I asked the Station Knob'ead,' she said, 'Do I get a refund?' Her friend took up the cause of all us fellow passengers by asking, 'You asked the Station Who?' 'You know,' came back the girl, 'The Station Knob'ead. That lad with the hat and the computer, behind the desk. The Station Knob'ead.' Despite the qualifying information, I still wasn't sure if this was an official job title.

In the evening sun, Stamford Bridge appeared gilded and felt close to quiet perfection. Villagers nursed pints outside The Bay Horse or watched the frothing weir behind the corn mill. On drowsy Viking Road and motionless Roman Avenue, all that could be heard were televisions through open windows and thrushes chatting to jackdaws in the wrong language. This was a place of totemic monkey puzzle trees, eggs for sale from drive-end boxes, water bowls for dogs by benches and a mini-library clamped to a limestone wall. Here was rural Yorkshire, a balm after the bedlam of Bradford and Leeds. Then the delayed fish and chip van bombed past, a whirlwind in a Quaker chapel.

Ever since John Rouse towed Dandy into Tommyfield Market there have been mobile fish and chip shops. First, donkeys or horses trailed carts from town to town, their coal-fired cauldrons and early ranges something of a portable fire hazard. Later, steam and then petrol engines were employed to move around caravan-like wagons, a flammable catastrophe still only a moment of ill-fortune or carelessness away. Hundreds were in operation by Edwardian times and from there technology and design advanced. Many had about them a certain artistry and bespoke charm. In 1930 the Paladini family of Dundee adapted a Cadillac touring car, welding on a 26-foot cream trailer marked 'The Travelling Restaurant'. The aim of this deluxe offering was to spread fish and chips out of the city and into new housing estates at its periphery. With its distinctive oval windows and visits announced by a loudspeaker attached to the American car's fenders, the future had arrived in the Dundonian schemes and it smelt wonderfully deep-fried.

Although novel to customers and often cherished, the existence of mobile chippies irked many in the traditional industry. Their proprietors were seen as bandits; highwaymen picking off customers wherever they chose and doing so while dodging the rules and rates that bricks and mortar fish and chip shops abided by. Mobile sellers also had a reputation for mooring their vans on the turf of established shops, sometimes right outside. With no rent to pay and low overheads, their prices were naturally cheaper. Redemption – or a truce at least – came during World War Two, when fish and chip trucks served urban evacuees the food they craved most in their countryside habitats.

Their numbers had peaked in the first half of the twentieth century, and as the years passed the sounds and smells of a mobile chip van were encountered less and less. In towns and villages where they did persist, they are remembered for their individuality, eccentricities and the occasional food poisoning anecdote. As with ice cream vans and, to some of us at least, mobile libraries, they represented something exciting, a break from the mundane. This weekly appearance was one of those inky blobs on the calendar marking something that makes life that little bit happier.

Joyfully, not all of them have disappeared. There are handsome campervan conversions to be found at street food events, wagons catering at fairs or football fixtures and traditional mobiles serving rural communities just as they have since horse and donkey days of yore. It was a version of the latter that I pursued now in Stamford Bridge.

The muffled clap of bat striking ball could be heard before I saw the village cricket ground entrance. Two young lads were engrossed in net practice, oblivious to the charms of Chippy's Traditional Fish & Chips van behind them. There, beyond the modern pavilion and beside the bowling club wall, locals were already clustered in a queue. Chippy's was yet to open and so the line grew, each new arrival offering a 'Now then, y'alright?' or a 'Hello Wendy, not seen you in a while, love.' Kids taking part in an impromptu multi-family game of cricket occasionally wandered over, each more violently *starving* than the last.

Some in the line had played in that afternoon's losing village team, more had watched and more still toddled over from the houses that encircle the pitch to meet the van, purses in hand. 'One of each, I'm having,' announced a genial man to no-one in particular, 'That's what they used to say. One fish and one chips.' It was a phrase I had completely forgotten, ditto the more Irish 'One and one,' both of them further linguistic tics sparked by the great dish.

A smiling lady in a catering tabard emerged from the back of the van. She greeted us all and then raised the hatch door. There were coos and the odd cheer, as if Mrs Chippy had pulled a curtain to reveal a prize wall. Instead, she had unveiled Steve, a cheery and kind-eyed man wearing bright blue rubber catering gloves. 'Ey up Steve lad,' came a buoyant cry. Pans were awoken and gurgled groggily then harmoniously. This was the closing chorus after a day's service across several now sated villages.

Mrs Chippy welcomed customers then took, prepared and called their orders while Steve soused fish in batter, prodded it to perfection, sieved ready items and tipped fresh chips from a colander into the pans. Every now and then, a countdown clock bleeped to denote that something had been fried to perfection, its call the very opposite of a weekday morning alarm. One such eruption provoked an enthused claim of, 'Oh, that must be my fish bites!' When that verdict was proved correct, the lady who made it gathered her bites and then raised each one to sparkle vinegar over the chips beneath it, a painstaking customisation. It was hot, hard work on the Chippy side and an entertaining performance from ours.

There was continuous dialogue between audience and performers. As Mrs Chippy ladled mushy peas into a foam vessel, a little girl asked if she could camp in the van one night. Steve enquired where another regular had been the previous week. 'I was in London, wasn't I?' came the reminder. 'Oh yeah,' said Steve in a concerned tone. 'Was it ok?' 'Better than I imagined,' offered the customer. A hearty man with tattoos of a different pet dog on each calf fetched the van workers' cold drinks from the bar. He also offered to transport the meals of struggling others: 'Need me to carry them for you, Maggie?' For once the word 'community' felt easy to define.

My turn came to declare for open over wrapped and then retreat from the van. In a cardboard raft, chips blond and tanned supported a fish that glowed in the setting sunshine. The batter looked almost pumpkin coloured, giving the meal an autumnal, harvest box serenity. I prised it open with a wooden fork and a puff of smoke climbed and then lingered, like that a steam train leaves in its wake. Laughter from the family cricket game hung in the empty sky, Steve's alarm sounded and mobile fish and chip shops suddenly seemed like the most civilised of all inventions.

Some 40 miles north, in Whitby, a Geordie day tripper spoke a sensible thought in an excitable tone. 'Oooh, I might get some chippies,' she said to her coach tour friends. 'Do any of youse mind?' No-one did and all three of them joined her. Close by on a noticeboard, an advertisement postcard written in spindly handwriting lamented, 'Due to back trouble I am selling all of my sea fishing tackle.' The card's calligraphy and trusting inclusion of a full home address told of an old person, one now involuntarily redundant from their pastime or even their occupation. Again, I reflected how gladness and sadness nestle close together when you are by the sea.

Whitby is never far from my thoughts. It is a crooked, magnetic, startling outpost of paradise. The air leaves me feeling soothed and the light sharpens outlines, like putting on a pair of glasses. The only good thing about leaving is that it means the next visit is closer. Yet this time its dreamy name had been blown into my ear by an unlikely cultural source: an ITV3 repeat of *Heartbeat*. In the episode I stumbled across, Claude Greengrass had purchased a mobile chippy for £175 from the Mazzetti family, a clan of Whitby-Italian fish and chip entrepreneurs who, judging by their mother's accent, hailed from the little-known Umbrian city of Swansea.

The episode made me realise that Whitby was, perhaps, the place I associated most with fish and chips. It is, and always had been since I could remember, impossible to visit this North Yorkshire town without eating from a chippy. Childhood visits meant stumpy pink sausages in waxy batter, and holidays trying a different chip shop each day. I ate chip shop food here with long-missed grandparents and with schoolfriends. Whitby fish and chips featured on the weekend my wife and I became engaged and are now the priority when we visit with our daughter. Although I adore curry, sitting in an Indian restaurant here one night I felt a sense of unease, or even guilt, as if I were sneakily drinking a can of lager in church. Whitby *is* fish and chips. And so I had to return.

From the foot of the 199 steps, I strolled by Arguments Yard and all the other ginnels and snickelways that twist out from its old cobbles. Through the pillars of the Old Town Hall, I spotted the shop that had been repurposed as Big Eddy's Chippy in the *Heartbeat* episode. Admittedly, this may not attract as many people to Whitby as does the town's association with Dracula. Then came the fibreglass polar bear, stretching in its usual berth on top of Holland & Barrett. It was put there in honour of a polar bear that the whale hunter William Scoresby had brought back to Whitby from a nineteenth-century expedition to Greenland. Kept as a pet, the bear swam in the very harbour I looked to now.

'Oh! It's a swinger!' shouted a lady behind me in a Brummie accent. Rather than making accusations of promiscuity at the bear or anyone else present, she referred to Whitby's Swing Bridge, operated as ever by a man sitting in a wooden hut. It was open now so that a fleet of boats could return from their day's fishing. Many of the vessels that leave Whitby's harbours do so for tourists, but many more still are working trawlers. It means that the waterside air here often rings with a collision of chip batter and engine diesel.

On the other side of the water, a man looked into the window of The Dracula Experience and shook his head. From amusement arcades came the tunes of machines competing with the chimes of raining coins. Ice cream stalls sold rock dummies on lanyards and Lemon Tops. A perfect fish and chips dessert, Lemon Tops are sold only between Redcar and Scarborough. The very thought of this delicacy's tart, toxically luminous yellow quiff of Whippy ice cream perching on a white pedestal of the same is enough to leave some of us from these parts weak at the knees. The Lemon Top appears to be hewn from North Yorkshire's coast; its contrasting shades and precipitous arrangement resemble the very cliffs it is served among. Freshly presented it is an object of beauty, the glowing Statue of Liberty torch of the North Riding.

A group of children sat in the bandstand eating their lunches while teachers prowled its circumference guarding against gulls. I looked at one of the local council's 'Stop attacks – never feed the gulls' posters and recalled the time I'd been doing the same when a man had shuffled up to me and said, 'It's all propaganda, that,' and then moved away again.

On the door of the Fish Market was another poster, promoting Muscular Skeletal Assessments for Active Fishermen. As in Brixham, it was a useful reminder of the brutally strenuous – physically and mentally – job that being a trawlerman is. Below, two such seafarers were unloading a catch, heaving bags of shellfish to the shore. A small public audience had assembled and now watched transfixed.

This country's obsession with the coast, the seaside town and all things nautical is an inevitable trait in an island nation. The ocean is part of our identity and therefore what comes from it, and the industries it births, are too. Fish and chips have almost inevitably been held up as a patriotic symbol since inception. Though written in a period when the dish was still resoundingly working-class and chippies regularly belittled, a syndicated 1924 newspaper column by 'P.A.S.' brimmed with these sentiments (as well as an unhealthy dose of racial stereotyping and language): 'It would not be too much to say, in sooth, that the British Lion's strength is largely built up on a combination of fried haddock and pieces of potato cooked in melted fat. Why? Nobody knows. It's like asking a man to explain why he smokes. He can't do it, any more than the inhabitants of Great Britain can explain why they can't get away from fish 'n' chips. Give the Frenchman his boiled frogs, and the Chinaman his toasted birds' nests, but whatever you do, don't take away our fish 'n' chips.'

It is, however, only in recent decades that fish and chips have become a widely accepted symbol of Britain. They are even a stereotype once again, though not now as a weapon with which to beat the poor, but as something representing all of us. That echoes, too, the idea that the meal has become classless and universal, even if chippies themselves remain blissfully idiosyncratic and varied. This may now be tested and strained by inevitable price rises – the working-class market which sustained fish and chips for its first century could soon be priced out, Chippy Night a rare treat rather than a familiar cry.

If there are few things more British than fish and chips (disregarding their origins and the nationalities of those who have often cooked them …), then *queuing* for fish and chips must buckle the scales of jingoism. The Magpie Café, opposite the boat by which I now stood, is famous for its elongated lines that stretch down towards the North Sea. It is *the* place to go in Whitby; the famous chip shop, the one guidebooks recommend and the celebrity chefs and reviewers swear by. The Magpie is on the seafront and by tradition costs a little more than Whitby's many other battered temples, but you wouldn't visit Paris and ignore the Eiffel Tower or Rome the Coliseum, would you? Apparently, my family would. Due to our rules, The Magpie was quarantined, a mysterious and unobtainable black and white château. Until now, I'd upheld those seaside traditions as outlined in Blackpool, and so this was to be my first visit.

The joys of queuing for fish and chips have littered these pages. From crossing the road led by nostrils towards a glowing refuge with its steamy windows, to joining up and deciding what to have, and then being overcome by an intensifying sense of anticipation, here is one of the great delights of chippy life. This would be my greatest queue yet, the longest wait repaid bounteously. I would talk about the people I'd met, the stories I'd heard in that Magpie line for years to come.

There was no queue.

Perhaps subconsciously yearning for a delay, I read the laminated menus outside. 'Whenever possible' my fish today would have been landed by WY ships *Victory Rose*, *Good Intent* or *Our Lass 3*. As 'Our Lass' is a term of endearment for a female partner round these parts, this would have been the moment when me and my new best friend in the queue could've speculated about whether there had been two previous ships or two previous wives. I had time to note that there were nine sandstone steps to the front door, suggesting that even just prior to the point of entry I was still hoping someone would wait behind me, tutting.

Inside The Magpie, this unknown pleasure and wild enigma, old floorboards creaked a hello echoed by merry staff. Rink-a-tink sounds of knives and forks on plates and teas being stirred drifted down from upstairs. There were ironwork magpie window guards and a frame displaying two aged illustrations of the birds on fragments of plasterboard. A staff member told me how these were salvaged from fires that had ravaged this place in 2017. 'Two for joy' must have seemed a cruel sentiment. The threat of frying range infernos has forever tortured this trade.

I asked where the Magpie name originated, expecting

some of Whitby's typical gothic darkness and necromancy. 'I've no idea,' she replied, giggling. 'Nobody seems to know. I've asked countless people and nobody has a clue. Not a clue!' It was just another of those fish and chip mysteries.

The couple on the table next to mine were going to order hake. 'We like to have something different every time we come,' said the man, 'and with the fire and Covid ... You know, you don't know how many visits you have left.' The Magpie was clearly a regular and a habit, and having fixtures and anchors matters to us all.

Knowing the answer already but wanting to hear it, at the end of my order I'd asked, 'And can I have some scraps please?' There was an indecipherable subplot in the way the waitress smiled and said 'Of course.' Now, as an overflowing cereal bowl of batter shards and specks was placed in front of me, I understood its meaning: This, lad, will be the greatest scrap experience of your life.

Beyond the vast portion size – there were easily enough to grit several B-roads – it is the temperature that I will always remember. It turns out that a mound of recently deep-fried atoms of batter is intensely hot. Pinching one of the larger pieces – which was shaped, incidentally, like the head and face of Mick Hucknall – in my fingers led me to immediately throw it down again as if it had bitten me. I spooned a few assorted tiny particles into my mouth, which provoked the kind of noise people usually make when they stand on a piece of Lego. Then, with a fork I scattered more scraps onto my chips while inexplicably muttering aloud, 'Oh yes. Oh yes please.' It was at this point that I noticed the hake couple shuffling their chairs further from my table. Possibly, the time had come to find someone to dine with.

Through a combination of ketchup, vinegar and time the scraps simmered enough for me to tuck in. It was like eating lush forkfuls of cake; crispy, greasy, heart-doctor-appalling cake. My scraps craving had, impossibly, been sated. We could all now move on until next time. As for the part of my meal that actually cost money – well, this was The Magpie, and it was everything people had said it was, if only we'd been listening. Cod in fence varnish gold batter pleased and lush chips calmed my scrap-hyper mouth. Leaving The Magpie behind, I bought a Lemon Top and walked to the end of the pier. Boats chugged out of the harbour and off to sea. Most turned north, as did I.

It was wartime on Tyneside and some of the boys were employing their gasmasks as footballs. Worse than that, said deputy chief air raid warden Mr F. J. Williams, 'I have heard that some have even used the masks to carry their nightly supply of fish and chips. This is a disgrace.' By that time, Francie Nichol of South Shields was fifty years old and no longer a chip shop owner. It was a shame; this indefatigable, engaging woman might well have laughed about it.

On this weekday afternoon, the redbrick grids that Francie once walked were hushed. It has been many years since the dockyards shouted over everything. Today, a lone door knock

in the next terrace could be heard and there were two unin-
habited moccasin shoes in the middle of Alice Street, as if
someone had spontaneously combusted in 1987 and no-one
had noticed. She had spent her days as an impoverished child
both here, and right down to the River Tyne and the North
Sea, 'Hawkin' fish and greens.' Those words, and Francie's
life, are documented in an extraordinary 1975 book by her
grandson Joe Robinson, *The Life and Times of Francie Nichol of
South Shields*.

In her young twenties, pretty and memorable in ornate
earrings and a knitted shawl, Francie had continued to sell
food before running lodging houses. Widowed at twenty-
four, she married again, this time to a vile man, Jack
O'Callaghan. O'Callaghan's mother owned a fish and chip
shop, which Francie worked in. Their family lived above it,
meaning that she was soon exploited and for nothing more
than a small wage. Jack, who was known for his tendency to
disappear, returned one night. 'He still hadn't got heself a
job. He was drinkin' like a fish and forever badly usin' us.
Takin' his hands to us at the slightest excuse.'

Francie understandably had her limit and argued with
O'Callaghan's mother, resulting in more violence. A local
businesswoman, Mrs Barnett, knew of the horrors Francie
endured. She offered this admirable young woman the funds
to set up a chip shop of her own.

Returning to the present day, I walked from Alice Street to
the corner of Gilbert and Frederick Streets, great rows of
intact two-up two-downs with their back lanes for bin wagons

and games of hide and seek. It was from here in 1917 that Francie would spy. The corner terrace shop that she fixed her eyes upon is now Bombay Babu takeaway. Then, it was a rundown old chippy and Francie's dream. Having put her children to bed, she would sneak out and stand for an hour to see who came and went, and indeed why it was failing so badly. 'I was jottin' down notes in me mind all the time,' she told Robinson, 'A drunk in the corner and two women with their arms spread over the counter, chattin' away. Same thing night after night. No way to run a business that wasn't.'

One night, Francie ventured inside. She was unimpressed: 'No proper pans or friers or anythin'. Tatey peelin's all over the floor. Two cats squabblin' over some fish in the back. No vinegar or pickles to be seen. The salt pot was dirty. The holes was closed up with grease, and it was empty into the bargain. The lino was worn away so ye could see the holes in the floorboards. Mice, almost certainly. Dead flies like blackberry jam in the little cracked window which was steamed up, and the fly-paper hangin' over the frier had too many flies in it.'

Having spat out the 'clay cold ... squelchy' chips she had bought, Francie waited until closing time and bid the owner 'Forty pound the lot, Missus!' Her offer was accepted, and the Barnetts provided a loan of £100 to cover the purchase and much-needed refurbishment costs. She had escaped the O'Callaghan hold, for now at least.

Francie transformed the shop, cleaning until it glimmered. She installed new equipment and bought fine ingredients, trekking to the fish market every morning herself. 'Drunks and lingerers' were barred and family customers enticed. Kids popped in for free scraps and returned with their mams for fish and chips. Francie also offered 'Tizer, pop and pickles. Beetroot, red cabbage and onions. Mussels and whelks.' All the labour was hers: 'I'd clean and gut the fish and peel and chip the tateys. Then I'd clean and fry, and sell and fry, and sell and fry and sell. All day and till late at night. And I enjoyed mesel.'

The business thrived. Her loan from the Barnetts was swiftly repaid. Where once the shop had taken less than a pound each day, now it was sometimes earning £20. Francie reinvested in the business ('I was the first woman in South Shields to put up a queue rail to control the customers comin' in and keep some kind of order') and saved £200 in 'A real bank account … Like all the rich people' had. Soon there were second and third Nichol fish and chip shops.

In the 1960s, Frederick Street was dissected by the A194 motorway, whose barrier wall I leaned against. I looked to the Indian takeaway and imagined Francie glancing back through her gleaming windows. Suddenly, a head appeared over the wall. 'Here, mate. Can you knock on her for me?' said a pale, near-toothless man who was somehow balancing on the crossbar of his bike. I gave a startled 'Pardon?' and he repeated himself. 'Knock on her for me, will yer, that door there?' He was pointing to Francie's old chippy. Spooked slightly, I made my excuses and headed back towards the moccasins. I walked to Walpole Street, the site of Francie's third chip shop. Here the bricks had no memories and the cobbles had been lifted – an industrial estate was planted over what once was another warren of terraces.

O'Callaghan's shadow – like his fists – had plagued Francie. He was prone to sitting in a pub opposite the first shop, raiding the till for his next Newcastle Brown, and borrowing money against the business. Francie bought him a chip shop, on Edith Street, so that he could drink away his own profits. It soon closed.

The Frederick Street shop was unable to take the strain of O'Callaghan's raids and went the same way in 1927. Walpole Street followed, so that by the thirties 'That was the end of that. No more fish and chip shop businesses for me.'

When Francie ran her business unencumbered, it flew. She was one of many women who found in the fish and chip trade a meritocratic space to thrive. That was simply not true of most other industries. To work in a chippy and then save to achieve ownership of one, or more, was a form of female liberation. Still, women would have to work harder than men, and men – often those from their own families – might try to thwart them. More widely, John K. Walton demonstrated how the role of women was 'systematically played down' by the industry's influential trade press. Yet here was an opportunity that had seldom existed before, and they took it. Clara, Francie and all those unsung others: the Champion Sisters of the Frying Range.

* * *

Later that day, I walked through Francie's world, passing pubs that were inadvertently her ruin. A man stumbled from the doorway of the imposing Trimmers Arms, here since 1891 and surely a haunt of O'Callaghan's. Then came the gallant Tyne, up from the banks of which her customers would trudge for a feed between shifts. At the market, women felt the fabric of trousers – 'Eee they'd do for wor Eddie, only £7 an' all. Canny, them like.' In their seesaw tones it was possible to imagine Francie's voice. Accents, like our love of fish and chips, pass almost without thought through the ages.

On Ocean Road, a man kissed the paws of a lion statue, his good luck ritual perhaps, as I walked towards Colman's chippy. The Colmans opened a fish and chip hut close to the beach here in 1905, and the modern restaurant remains in the family, although it is the kind of institution that locals feel *they* own. As we have seen, chippies are often started by and then passed through families. That same pattern is replicated in their customers: we go here because grandad loved it or there because it tastes like it always has. We are part of the lineage, the tradition.

At the entrance to Colman's there was a boxy holding porch in which diners waited. Its double doors faced on to the restaurant, and once I'd been seated I watched various inmates come and go. It resembled one of those glass chambers that Russian dissidents stand in when on trial in Moscow. There was more glass next to me; a beautiful, mammoth fish tank above which a vibrantly festooned fishing net was affixed to the ceiling. Around the corner hung a photograph gallery of famous visitors, including John Major, Tony Blair and, more excitingly, Vera Duckworth from Corrie. I am a big fan of restaurants using these images, though wonder what the criteria for inclusion is, and whether minor celebrities slightly lower down the pecking order spend a great deal of their meal time nervously hoping to be asked for a photo. Mind, I was once in a small-town curry house that included a local GP, so the barrier isn't always that high.

Next to me, two nanas made competing claims about their grandchildren. These were not always of a positive nature and included a disagreement about which of them had the worst allergies. Just as a waitress placed down my fish-shaped plate, one of them added, 'If he doesn't take them pills, he gets the runs. If he does take them, he gets bunged up. We canna win.'

I doused my cod and chips in vinegar, perhaps hoping the tart scent would force a change of subject from them or a bout of temporary amnesia in me. Luckily the fish, shaped like a narrow oven glove, was one of the best I'd had. It possessed that volcanic rush of heat with the ability to reverse the years. Parts of the chips had a crispy veneer that resembled an ice-glazed puddle. And it turned out that I was ready for scraps again.

All through the meal, if only to shut out the competitive grannies, I reflected on the last couple of months. Important lessons had been learned: the most southerly scraps were in the Rhondda Valley, and as I'd had scraps in Norfolk on a previous trip, we can unsafely, unscientifically assert that the Southern Scraps Border runs diagonally from Cardiff to Norwich.

I had found tremendous gratification in visiting or even just seeing so many living, breathing chip shops in all their individuality. This is an expensive, back-breaking type of business to run, one from which actual battle scars are incurred – the arms of many a fryer are pocked with oil blots and dripping lesions. Yet still they remain, 8,000 or 9,000 chippies, no two identical or serving exactly the same food. Love goes into this trade, from both sides of the counter.

There is depth to what chip shops have contributed, as the great themes of social class, war, immigration, identity and women's liberation have demonstrated. They are smaller than that, too, and that is no offensive slight; chippies mean so much to individuals and communities. They are reliable, safe, constant, comforting, homely, funny and human. Fish and chips say unifying things about us – Britain – as a whole, but also can feel specifically personal and *ours* (look at the way we all know how best to customise them with salt, vinegar and even gravy).

From Dundonian grumps to a bourgeois balcony in Devon, in their own ways I have loved them all. You should too. They are one of the best things about us.

ENDPIECE

The Perfect Fish and Chips

Some weeks after my travels ended, a friend asked what had been the finest fish and chips I'd eaten and which chippies I'd loved most. Instead of offering a sharp and straight answer, I found myself volunteering certain attributes and moments from different places and meals – the way that steamy haze ascended from a Blackpool cod; scrumpy Welsh chips on a sun-capped wall ...

These thoughts flowed into the kind of whimsical, illusory conversation that happens all too rarely as years elapse and mates begin to talk of mortgages rather than which animals they could 'take' in a fight. Soon, we found ourselves setting out the exact environment, conditions and ingredients for our perfect chippy tea – like Orwell's 'Moon Under Water' only with slightly more Sarson's vinegar. Mine went a little like this ...

It would have to be an autumn or early winter's evening, dry and windless and cold enough for breath to be visible but not so cold as to induce numb toes. To eat on a summer's afternoon is amply pleasant but lacks the hurtling electric chemistry of hot food colliding with chilly air, that saintly chain reaction. This darkness would also allow my chip shop to glow lustrously, an irresistible invitation to cross the road. Also present in that splendid window: a neon 'Open' – or even 'Frying Tonight' – sign winking seductively. And throughout a sedate twilight such as this, the chippy's bewitching aromas could be found loitering in the air with no cause to move on, a welcome occupation that makes stomachs sigh longingly.

Six or seven people would be lingering on the pavement outside, waiting for their orders to be shouted like game-show contestants hoping for the host's call. 'Are you in the queue?' I'd be forced to ask, sparking a polite 'No, sorry mate.' Our doorway offers a warm current of searing batter and sturdy vinegar at the point of joining the real queue, a happy but arms-free conga line whose members dance imperceptibly to the music of the frying pans.

There is a voice from the back of the shop: 'Any fish for you tonight?' bellows a man dressed in a cricket umpire's coat and pointing over with the mesh fish skimmer gripped in his hand. In my utopian chippy, no haddock or cod is left to shrivel and diminish over several hours of service. All fish is fried *now*, even if that means hanging around outside like bike shed ciggie kids, half-convinced they've forgotten our order.

Though steadfastly concentrating on several tasks at once, the umpire's colleagues would bring this place's cheer with their gossipy catch-ups over the range ('Is your John still in hospital, Elsie?') and their polite chitchat with passing strangers ('Have you been at the match, flower?') From their mouths flow the vital questions of 'Salt and vinegar?', 'Open or wrapped?' and all the rest. They await customer responses with the kindly concern of parish vicars.

My chippy would have no café or sit-in area. The only cutlery here is wooden. This means simplicity but also a cosy, relatively small and immersive operation. Warmth from the frying range heats a customer's front as they lean their back against a Formica wall in blotchy pale yellow, unchanged since the umpire's mum and dad kept the shop.

When not embroiled in the tittle-tattle of the queue, there are other things to concentrate upon: the chrome splendour of the range with its manufacturer's name badge and declaration of having been made in some steady town like Preston or Halifax; timeless posters championing a certain brand of sausage or heralding 'Fish & Chips: The Great British Takeaway'; a homespun, analogue menu board of sallow but once-white letters pinned into holes on a black plastic board and surrounded by a constellation of fluorescent labels offering 'Vimto 80p' and 'Ketchup Sachets 20p'.

From that board, my order is simple: cod and chips and scraps, all fried in beef dripping. Nothing else possesses the depth of taste it gives, nor the textures it unleashes and the stout but brittle batter it forges. Cod has a lightness not always guaranteed with haddock, plus the latter carries a risk of arriving with skin intact, thus riling the ghost of my grandad. The chips from this pocket of heaven have a little crunch in them and are almost amber in colour. By way of coronation, salt and vinegar are scattered throughout and tomato sauce – hopefully Daddy's Ketchup or some other lesser-spotted breed – dolloped in a corner.

All of this perfection is cradled in half-a-dozen sheets of off-white paper, allowing condiments to stay balanced on their hosts and not become absorbed by card or polystyrene. From this bundle scents escape and push a smile across their new owner's face, eyes closed in besotted anticipation. A can of Dandelion and Burdock rests in my coat pocket and I am ready to find a wall to eat upon, lap heated and vapours rising towards the stars.

TOP 10 CHIPPY MOMENTS

An autobiographical breeze through ten chippies that mean the most to me.

1. Bill's, Copmanthorpe. The village chippy where it all began, pressing my face on the steamy range window and awaiting the crumbly, bumpy batter.
2. Essex Street, Middlesbrough. Me and Dad, the cold disappointment of a Boro game at Ayresome Park and then the hot glee of post-match dusky gold chips from a terraced house.
3. Wetherby Whaler, York. Teenage times and Mum introduces Tuesday Treat Night to colour that bland day – there are pizzas and curry, but nothing so glorious as choosing the Whaler.
4. Wetherby Whaler, Wetherby. The original, smooth batter and chips with a week's worth of flavour; contented memories of Grandma Gray taking half of hers home for an oven reheat.

5. Miller's, York. The gang that met in a village playgroup is about to split – one last meal on A-level results night, one last chance for scrap butties and pointless, happy arguments.

6. Clayton Street Chippy, Newcastle. Wandering the rainy streets far from home. Leaving for university is a lonely thing, then comes the glow of a chip shop and that homely taste.

7. Tail End, Leith. This tiny young thing of epic blue eyes decides that fish and chips are our daddy and daughter meal, Tail End our den; giggles at the mouth contortions vinegar makes.

8. Pinnacles, Seahouses. Holiday fish and chips are the best fish and chips and we found ours by the North Sea. First came the throwback decor and Panda Pops of Pinnacles. Then …

9. Silver Street Fisheries, Whitby. A backyard chippy down an alley off a side street, almost, with high palatial windows and fish and chips conjured in a dream.

10. Bertie's, Edinburgh. Our now place, bold and large and far from historic but here good times roll and angelic fish and chips fill up our senses.

SELECT BIBLIOGRAPHY

Gerald Priestland, *Frying Tonight: The Saga of Fish & Chips* (Gentry Books, 1972)

Joe Robinson, *The Life and Times of Francie Nichol of South Shields* (Futura, 1977)

Joe Pieri, *The Scots-Italians: Recollections of an Immigrant* (Mercat Press, 2005)

John K. Walton, *Fish & Chips & the British Working Class, 1870–1940* (Leicester University Press, 1992)

Panikos Panayi, *Fish and Chips: A Takeaway History* (Reaktion Books, 2022)

ACKNOWLEDGEMENTS

Enormous gratitude to my agent, David Luxton, for his belief in me, and to everyone at DLA. The same to Jonathan de Peyer at HarperNorth, who has been an extremely supportive and creative editor to work with, and to his friendly colleagues there; the chips with scraps – or whatever you call them on the dark side of the Pennines – are on me next time I'm in town. As ever, it would be impossible for me to write anything without the love and understanding of Marisa and Kaitlyn, or without everything my parents have given me, from the chippy queue onwards. Finally, this book only exists because of the fine and unstoppable breed who make the batter and stack the pop: chip shop workers of the world, you have my deepest thanks and those of a million and more others.

Harper North

BOOK CREDITS

HarperNorth would like to thank the following staff and contributors for their involvement in making this book a reality:

Fionnuala Barrett
Samuel Birkett
Peter Borcsok
Ciara Briggs
Sarah Burke
Matthew Burne
Alan Cracknell
Jonathan de Peyer
Anna Derkacz
Morgan Dun-Campbell
Tom Dunstan
Kate Elton
Sarah Emsley
Simon Gerratt
Monica Green
Natassa Hadjinicolaou
Megan Jones

Jean-Marie Kelly
Taslima Khatun
Sammy Luton
Rachel McCarron
Molly McNevin
Petra Moll
Alice Murphy-Pyle
Adam Murray
Genevieve Pegg
Agnes Rigou
James Ryan
Florence Shepherd
Eleanor Slater
Emma Sullivan
Katrina Troy
Daisy Watt

For more unmissable reads,
sign up to the HarperNorth newsletter at
www.harpernorth.co.uk

or find us on Twitter at
@HarperNorthUK

**Harper
North**